Focs'le Days

A Story of my Youth

Focs'le Days

A Story of my Youth

ANTON OTTO FISCHER

WITH PAINTINGS BY THE AUTHOR

Hudson River Maritime Center
Kingston, NY
1987

ACKNOWLEDGEMENTS

Klock Kingston Foundation
Henry P. Kendall Foundation

Gertrude W. Anderson (Mrs. Bev Anderson)
Wiggie & Tony DeLisio and children
Fred C. Doty (and IBM Matching Funds Program)
Katrina Sigsbee Fischer
Rose-Marie Forst Lewent
Dorothy & S. James Matthews

Special thanks to all other contributors.

Published by the Hudson River Maritime Center, One Rondout Landing, Kingston, New York 12401.

Designed by Christine Miller.
Produced by Joanna Hess and Bryan McHugh.

LLCN 87-082667
ISBN 0-940769-01-8

Manufactured in the United States of America.

this book is dedicated
to all the boys
young and old
who love the sea and ships

CONTENTS

ILLUSTRATIONS

FOREWORD

"FOCS'LE DAYS" did not start out as a written book. A good many years ago the idea came to me to make a pictorial account of life at sea in the days of the old sailing ships. I planned to show in two or three dozen pictures the action, drama, humor and not infrequent tragedy which made up the life of the deep-water sailor. But for my wife and daughter it might have remained just an idea. Through their persistence I finally painted four of the subjects I had in mind. I soon discovered, however, that the cost of making color plates was considered prohibitive. One publisher showed a mild interest in the project, but he thought an explanatory text absolutely essential. I am not a writer, and "Focs'le Days" almost died in its inception right then and there. When World War II broke out I shelved the unsatisfactory attempts I had made, but at the end of the year my interest revived, and encouraged by my wife's advice to forget literature and just write as I used to tell the yarns to our children and friends, the book became a reality. For me to write a true picture of the life in a tramp sailing ship's focs'le, the story necessarily had to be told autobiographically. That naturally limited the pictures I had planned.

The living and working conditions on the old sailing ships were very different from the comparatively comfortable life on the modern steamships of today, but I don't agree at all with the old sailor's usually patronizing attitude toward the modern sailor. They are no less hardy a breed. It took the same stamina to man the ships carrying war cargoes through the submarine-infested North Atlantic convoy routes, and around the North Cape to Murmansk, as to fight gales and blizzards off Cape Horn, and I personally would much rather fight a stubborn, frozen topsail on a sleet-covered yard than to try to get away from a torpedoed tanker through a sea covered with burning oil. I think the reader will agree, when he finishes this book, that any improvement in conditions was long overdue.

I want to express my deep appreciation of my daughter's loyal co-operation and assistance with the text. In some ways it is almost as much her book as mine.

Preface to Second Edition

I first read *Focs'le Days* twelve years ago when my then husband-to-be, Andre Mele, presented me with a very worn copy of the book. Anton Otto Fischer was his uncle and we were in the stage of courtship when I was being introduced to his family. I loved the book, as so many have, and regretted that I missed meeting the author by many years. I remember remarking what a pity it was that the book was out of print. Since that time, professional affiliation and good luck have brought me to a position where I can participate in the reprinting of *Focs'le Days* which Scribner's first published in 1947.

We have worked faithfully to reproduce the original book, changing as little as possible. The first edition had such an appealing format that it seemed wise not to tinker with a good thing. A notable and interesting addition is the print of an early picture of the *Gwydyr Castle* painted in 1901 when AOF was a very young man.

The purpose of the project has been to make this enduring story available not only to an audience already familiar with his work, but to a whole new generation who dream of the sea and the adventures that were to be had aboard a square rigger. The paperback version will make the book affordable to a wider audience, and the use of color illustrations will give the reader a better feeling for the quality and drama of the original paintings.

Some of you may wonder why a museum on the Hudson River in Kingston is publishing a "deep water" book (Karl Kartum wondered about this aloud over lunch a couple of years ago while he was trying to obtain the book from Katrina Fischer for the National Maritime Museum at San Francisco). Outside of the aforementioned familial ties, it should be remembered that AOF left the sea and made his home port up river in the mountains. He resided in Kingston for twelve years and made many friends here. In 1982 the Hudson River Maritime Center put on an exhibition of his paintings entitled *Anton Otto Fischer: Marine Artist* as one of the museum's early efforts to establish itself in the region. The show was attended by people from far and wide, but a dedicated group of Kingston Fischer fans flocked in as well. Many a mantel in Kingston is graced by an AOF marine painting, not to mention the many landscapes for which he is equally well known. With a couple of exceptions, the funding for this project came from people in the community who knew and loved his work.

The publication of this wonderful book calls for thanks to the following people: Katrina Fischer for allowing us to reprint her father's book and for donating all the proceeds from the sale of *Focs'le Days* to the museum; Alan R. Bendelius, former president of the Hudson River Maritime Center, who always encouraged and supported me in undertakings such as this; William Spangenberger, board member and chairman of the *Focs'le Days* Committee, for his fund raising efforts; Earle Foster, a trustee of the Klock Kingston Foundation, for their major commitment to the project; Charmi Neely for coordinating the production; and, of course, my husband Andre Mele for introducing me to AOF.

Marita Lopez-Mena
Executive Director, Hudson River Maritime Center, Kingston, NY

INTRODUCTION

THE SEA has always had a strange fascination for boys of an adventurous bent. Some had the sea in their blood by heritage and tradition. To others it meant romance and adventure; to others again, it was an escape.

The sea made no irresistible call to me. I came from a line of forebears who for generations had cultivated the same plot of land on a highland plateau in the hills of Bavaria. Going to sea never entered my mind at all, though I was at the time very unhappy and was desperately searching to find a way out from a situation and a set of circumstances beyond my control. And suddenly fate opened the door for me and showed me the way to escape.

At the time I was a printer's devil on *Der Bayerische Volksbote,* a clerical newspaper published in Regensburg, Bavaria. My foreman had sent me out on an errand and I was making my way back to the shop. It was a raw, drizzly January morning in the year 1898, and the atmosphere was quite in keeping with my state of mind. I hated the shop, and the foreman, and I hated the home in which I lived. Suddenly turning from a side alley into the main street, my eye was arrested by the sight of a large poster in the window of a travel agency. As if drawn by a magnet I approached the window, and stood, oblivious of the chilling drizzle, the shop, and my errand. The poster showed a sailing ship scudding along under full sail, with wind-driven clouds revealing a blue sky over an ultramarine sea. White gulls circled the ship, adding enchantment to the scene. The world around me disappeared. Free as one of the gulls, I was sailing on such a ship to foreign lands. Reluctantly I tore myself away from my dream and returned to the shop, to be greeted with a cuff on the head for my tardiness, but I couldn't get the vision of that ship out of my head all day, and when the shop closed I returned to the poster before I went back to the narrow alley along the Danube where I lived as an unwelcome addition to my uncle's house.

My uncle was my legal guardian but neither he, nor especially his wife, had thought of the possibility that they might at some time be saddled with me. They resented the fact that I had deliberately forfeited what seemed to them a remarkable opportunity for an honorable and bright future. My mother, against the combined opposition of her family, had married my father, an upholsterer. There were two children, my sister and myself. My father died of occupational tuberculosis when I was a little over three years of age and my sister still an infant in arms. My mother had a hard time keeping her family together, and after a year of struggle with poverty and illness, died of the same disease. During the year of her widowhood her plight came to the attention of a Baroness von L——who eased her predicament in many ways, and enabled her to find such needlework as she could do at home. When my mother's end approached her benefactress eased her last hours by promising that my sister and I would be taken care of.

On her death my sister was immediately placed for adoption and I was put temporarily with an elderly cobbler and his wife.

When I was five years old, through the influence of Baroness von L——, a patroness of the institution, I was placed in the orphan asylum at Indersdorf conducted by the Sisters of the Order of St. Vincent of Paul. Baroness von L——was a devout Catholic and her ultimate plans for me were the priesthood. I spent the years 1887 to 1894 in that institution. I did very well in school and was also taught the piano. Baroness von L——must have received good reports about me, because preparations were made to have me admitted into the Archiepiscopal Seminary of Scheyern. During my seventh year in grade school I was prepared for the entrance examination and did so well I was admitted into the second year of Latin. Scheyern is a Benedictine monastery. The Paters were very kind, but the discipline was strict and it wasn't long before I ran into difficulties. I hadn't the slightest inclination to become a priest, and was constantly in trouble until it became only too evident to the monks themselves that I had no vocation for the priesthood.

Then Baroness von L——died, and I lost the one person who had shown a personal interest in me. I became more aware that I was an object of charity and my resentment showed itself in an increasingly rebellious attitude. I was a difficult, moody boy and given to attacks of senseless rage that left me physically exhausted. One afternoon in a moment of desperation I burst into the Abbot's room, threw myself down in front of him and begged to be allowed to go away, anywhere at all. The Abbot was a very kind and understanding man. He put his hand on my head and told me the Fathers had long ago realized I was not suited to the priesthood, but where could they send me? I sobbed that perhaps I could study art instead of theology, so arrangements were made for me to travel to Munich to call on Baron von L——with a portfolio of drawings. The Baron by this time received so many unfavorable reports about me he was inclined to show no further interest, but he took me to the studio of an artist friend to whom I showed my drawings. His opinion was unfavorable, and that was the end. I returned to the Seminary in the depths of despair.

The Fathers thought it useless to keep me any longer and got in touch with my uncle, who reluctantly agreed to take me in. It was a far from warm welcome I received, and in fact, on the part of my aunt, was even venomous. Due to my seminary background my uncle was able to place me as printer's devil on the clerical newspaper, but the stay with my uncle was the unhappiest period of my life. There again I was eating of the bread of charity. At Indersdorf and Scheyern the charity was impersonal, and Sister Philomena and Sister Arcadia and Pater Anselm and Pater Ulrich occasionally showed me affection, but in my uncle's house the attitude was bitter and resentful towards me. I was crying for escape, but until fate led me past that travel agency window, I didn't know whereto.

It took me quite a while to summon the courage to broach the subject of going to sea to my uncle, but one particularly bad day at the shop made up my mind, and that evening I asked my uncle to let me go. He thought I had gone crazy. It was out of the question. As *Braumeister* of the principal brewery in Regensburg, he had a position to maintain, and could not invite the criticism and gossip which getting rid of me in such an extraordinary fashion would arouse. There followed weeks of a tug of war between his refusal and my growing determination to get away at any cost. Regensburg is the final port for all up-river traffic on the Danube, and I haunted the quaysides watching Hungarian tugs and barges, often tempted to stow myself on one of them in spite of their lack of romance. One day I got an idea how to break down my uncle's resistance. I was setting type for a paragraph telling of the suicide attempt of a young girl. Why not stage a suicide attempt! The more I thought of it, the more the idea appealed to me. I was familiar with the banks of the Danube, and my uncle's house was situated close to the river. Along its banks were coal yards and warehouses and there were always men and facilities for rescue handy. One morning I left the shop and walked down to the river. I strolled up and down a few times to attract the attention of two men near by, and then jumped. I could swim, but I had underestimated the current, and was rapidly carried downstream. However, the people on the bank had gotten busy, and with a long hook kept ready for emergencies I was fished out, wrapped in blankets and deposited over a near-by baker's oven to thaw out. I wasn't prepared for the notoriety which followed, and began to realize I had done my uncle an ill turn indeed. But the escapade served its purpose, and he gave his consent to my going to sea. His final words to me were that I had made my bed, and could lie in it. There was to be no returning if things turned out badly. We said good-by at

the railroad station, and that was the last we ever saw of each other.

My uncle had given me the address of a sailor's boarding house in the St. Pauli section of Hamburg. He had forwarded the proprietor enough money to pay for my board until a berth as deck boy could be found for me, and to outfit me with the things I needed for life aboard ship. The boardinghouse keeper was a kindly, honest man and I was in good hands. The day after my arrival I hurried to the waterfront to watch the activity. It was all strange to me, and my imagination saw nothing but romance and adventure. There were tall-masted ships; strange odors; seamen of all nationalities and races, white, yellow and black; a big incoming steamer; a four-masted ship in tow of a tug going down the river to sea; gulls circling and crying, and small craft everywhere like busy water beetles. I watched fascinated until evening and hunger drove me back to the boarding house. The following day the boardinghouse keeper took me shopping for an outfit of woolen underwear, shirts, socks and a stout pair of sea boots, pea jacket, cap, oilskins and southwester. I was thrilled when he thought I needed a sheath-knife. I had a little pocket money, so I invested in a pipe and some shag tobacco, in which I immediately lost interest after the first pipeful. The next day, dressed the way a sailor ought to look, in turtleneck sweater, visored cap and sheath-knife ostentatiously displayed, I returned to the waterfront clenching a cold pipe between my teeth, hoping to be taken for a sailor from one of those tall ships crowding the docks.

One of the boarders was a sailor just paid off after a voyage from Calcutta. He told me enthralling yarns of the sea and foreign ports, until my impatience to exchange the status of a would-be sailor for the real thing was fanned to a fever pitch. Finally one day at supper the boardinghouse keeper announced that a ship had been found for me. I was to take the train the next morning to a place called Horumersiel where the ship was getting ready for a trip to Norway. I knew of Hamburg, Bremen, Luebeck, Stettin, but Horumersiel? He was rather evasive as to details, but my enthusiasm wasn't dampened one whit. In the morning the boardinghouse keeper put me on the right train and gave me the few marks left from the money my uncle had sent him. I was on my own, and suddenly felt very much alone in the world. The coach was crowded with passengers, all of whom spoke Platt-Deutsch, and I couldn't understand a word. The monotonous, drab countryside going by was very different from my vivid Bavarian homeland, and reaction took hold of my spirits.

At last the conductor touched me on the shoulder, and from the familiar word "Horumersiel" in his remarks I gathered we were almost there. When the train stopped I descended, dragging my seabag after me. A small building served as the station and the only people in sight were three old codgers grouped at one end of the building. One of them, a wizened little man with a clipped gray chin beard came over to where I stood. I couldn't understand a word he said, so he pointed to my sea bag and beckoned to me to follow him. We took a road that led apparently nowhere. My eyes kept roving over the flat landscape. You could see miles in every direction, but nowhere was the skyline broken by the tall masts of a ship. The old fellow made no more attempts at conversation and we plodded along silently. Finally we turned into a grassy lane that went off to the right, and presently came upon some pilings driven

into the mud. There, lying heeled over on a mud flat, was a small galleass. The tide was out and gulls were circling around us and feeding in the mud, their raucous cries like mocking laughter at the collapse of my dreams. This couldn't be my ship! It wasn't possible! This clumsy-looking barge with its rounded bluff bow and a mudboard on either side! I dropped my bag on the ground and stood there, stricken with a sickening disappointment. A couple of planks led down from the piling to the slanting deck of the galleass and the old man descended on deck motioning me to follow him. A big, red-bearded man emerged from the tiny deckhouse and engaged him in animated conversation, looking and pointing at me, then he took my sea bag and threw it on one of the bunks in the deck-house, which was a tiny cubicle half sunk into the deck. It contained space for two bunks, a provision locker, and, in the forward part, space for spare sails and cordage. It was about four feet in height, just comfortable to sit in. There was a small cook stove, as it also served as the galley, and the supper of sowbelly, cowpeas, and a kettle of tea was simmering on the stove. The old man was the captain, and had his quarters belowdeck in the stern of the ship. A tiny hatch led down to it. The captain was also the owner of the galleass. Her name was the *Renskea* and she carried three men, the captain, the mate and a deckhand. I was the deckhand, and also the cook. She was a small vessel of thirty-three tons engaged principally in the lumber trade between Norwegian and East Friesian ports.

We all sat down around the stove and the captain dished out three platefuls, but I was still in a daze and couldn't eat. The mere sight of food, combined with the mixed odors of cooking, tar, and mud threatened to nauseate me. The red-bearded man coaxed me finally to take some tea as a bracer, but the first swallow of that unfamiliar bitter black brew produced a spasm of nausea and I stumbled out onto the slanting deck and almost fell overboard into the mud. The reaction had been too much for me. But if the *Renskea* was a sorry answer to my dreams, I was no bonanza to the old captain and the mate. My ignorance of anything dealing with ships and life at sea was abysmal, and I still remember my consternation when I discovered that ships didn't drop anchor every night, but sailed right on.

The next morning the mate roused me at dawn and showed me how to make the fire. The tide was coming in, and at high tide we would leave the slip and be on our way to Krageroe, Norway. As soon as we were under way I was told to put on the cowpeas for the noonday meal. This I did, but unfortunately I used sea water from over the side so the peas refused to soften up. The captain was furious, but by that time the little galleass had begun to respond to the action of the small waves in the bay, and the almost imperceptible motion already made me queasy. As we approached open water the action became more pronounced, and I succumbed completely. I never wanted to see the inside of the deck-house again and curled up in the scuppers, indifferent as to whether I was washed or kicked overboard. I was utterly useless on that trip, but one frosty morning the snow-clad coast of Norway appeared on our starboard bow and the sight had a magical effect on me. For the first time in over a week I showed an interest in food, and when we sailed into the placid waters of Krageroe harbor, I was up and around, trying to be as useful as my ignorance would let me be. Both the cap-

tain and the mate were intrinsically kind men, and when I turned to with a will, they were willing to forgive and forget, in the hope I would prove a useful hand yet. I never conquered my tendency to seasickness while on the *Renskea*, but after that first trip it never incapacitated me. I was always able to do the necessary work on deck, and gradually became used to the food which, though coarse, was wholesome and plentiful. We made altogether three voyages to Norway, and I always enjoyed the stay in Krageroe. I never went ashore, but I could always have the dinghy to go off fishing. The water was incredibly clear in the harbor and the fishing good fun in amongst the kelp-covered rocks.

The little galleass was chartered by a merchant and dealer in building supplies to bring logs to Horumersiel. The logs were brought to our bow on rafts, and then snaked into our hold through two portholes. There was no additional help and the mate and I loaded and stowed the entire cargo by ourselves. It was hard work, and not with out a certain amount of danger, but I thoroughly enjoyed it and worked hard, if for no other reason than to prove that I was of some use after all. My wages were ten marks or two dollars and fifty cents a month, and while in port I really earned them.

In Krageroe, on the first trip, my morale had been so low, I wrote my uncle asking to be allowed to come home. Back in Horumersiel I received the reply. It was a kind letter, but my request was denied. By that time I was sorry I had written the letter at all, and the refusal left me indifferent. I was at last on the way to independence. In Horumersiel I became acquainted with the merchant who chartered the galleass. He was a widower with two young daughters of ten and twelve.

They came down to the vessel with their father and we became good friends, so much so that several times I was asked to supper at their house. The merchant also asked me to come and see him when the *Renskea* was tied up for the winter. As the months went by I acquired self-confidence, and while the life of a sailor had lost its glamour, I appreciated my independence and was convinced that now I could always make my way unaided. It was late in the year when the *Renskea* arrived in Horumersiel at the end of her third and last trip from Krageroe. When the cargo was discharged, I was paid off, and received a little over sixty-five marks or sixteen dollars for my eight months' work. I had no plans, but the money would not see me through the entire winter, so I called on the merchant to remind him of his invitation. He and his family were very glad to see me, and I was asked to spend the winter months with them. There were many ways in which I could make myself useful and I spent the entire winter keeping accounts, tutoring the two girls, working around the yard and occasionally driving his four-horse teams to Wilhelmshaven and other outlying towns. I received no pay, but was treated like a member of the family, and the friendship and companionship of his daughters more than compensated me. I was happier with them than I had ever been before.

When spring arrived I became restless and was torn between the desire to stay with the merchant's family and the urge to go to sea again. When I told the merchant I wanted to go back to sea he said I knew best what I wanted, but that I could always come back if I changed my mind. He gave me my ticket to Bremerhaven, and a small sum of money to tide me over until I found a ship. My last sight of the family was of the two girls waving frantically as the train pulled out. I went to a sailors' boarding house in Bremerhaven and haunted the waterfront for a possible berth as deck boy. One day I came on a Norwegian barque discharging a cargo of ice, and on impulse went aboard to ask whether they could use a deck boy. The skipper questioned me, with his German-speaking wife who lived on board acting as interpreter, and the interview ended by my being signed on as an ordinary seaman. The barque was named *Agustina* and hailed from Christiania, now called Oslo. She was a beautiful ship and more like the ship of my earlier dreams. I was very happy on her and the captain's wife, who was childless, treated me almost like an adopted son. But for the fact that I was only a boy, it might have caused resentment towards me amongst my shipmates. The crew was mostly Norwegian with a sprinkling of Russian Finns. The food was plentiful and of excellent quality, and the lift in my morale was such that I was never again seasick.

We left Bremerhaven with a cargo of coke for Kronstadt, the Russian naval base, and from there went to Kotka, Finland, to take on a cargo of lumber for London. We made three voyages between Kotka and English ports, always carrying lumber. On the third and last trip the ship struck a reef in the Baltic and became waterlogged. A Swedish torpedo boat came to our rescue and towed us into Karlskrona, the Swedish naval base, where the damage was found to be so great that the crew was discharged. I was kept on for a couple of months as night watchman, but then became restless, and on hearing of a Swedish coastal steamer leaving for Russian Baltic ports and eventually Hamburg I asked the captain of the *Agustina* for my discharge, and signed on a Swedish steamer. She was named *Ruth* and her home port was Goteborg. I intended to stay on her only long enough to get to Hamburg, and after a terrifying incident with a half-witted shipmate, whose death grip on my throat I finally loosened by pressing him back against the red-hot focs'le stove, I was glad to leave her. In Hamburg I took lodgings in a sailors' boarding house, and there I met a fisherman of the North Sea trawler fleet who was convalescing from some injuries. We became good friends and when he was ready to go to sea again we both signed on his former trawler, the *Schillighorn*. I spent most of the winter on her, fishing in the North Sea and the Baltic. The experience did more to harden me as a sailor than anything that had gone before. The Danish skipper was a hard taskmaster but worked like one of the crew. He never spared us nor himself. Through gales and bitter cold the fishing went on like clockwork. The trawls were hauled in every eight hours, emptied on deck and set again. Then came the task of gutting, cleaning and storing the fish below, often in temperatures close to zero. Finally the backs of my hands and forearms became such a mass of running sores that I had to stay ashore to get medical attention. When they were healed I looked around again for something to do.

The Boer War was then in full swing, and my sympathy, like most sailors' other than British, was all with the Boers. I tried to find a berth on a steamer of the Woerman Line, a German steamship company trading with South African ports, intending to desert in South Africa and join the Boers, but fate had other plans. I had no luck with the Woerman Line, but finally found a berth as ordinary seaman on a steamer of the Levant Line which traded between Hamburg, Rotterdam, Antwerp and Mediterranean and Black Sea ports. All the ships of that line were named after the islands of the Greek Archipelago, and my ship was the *Chios*. For the first time since I had gone to sea the romance of foreign places entered into my activities. Malta, Algiers, Saloniki, Constantinople, Odessa, Batum, Galatz, Novorosisk and numerous other smaller ports along the Turkish and North African coasts all meant the mystery of the Levant to me. I made three round trips on the *Chios* through the Mediterranean to the Black Sea. On our last trip we reached Rotterdam in the midst of a continental longshoreman and sailors strike. With some difficulty we discharged such cargo as was destined for that port, and left for our home port of Hamburg, where I was paid off along with most of the crew. Due to the strike, ships were hard to find, but I found temporary employment on a seagoing tug called *Blitz*, lured by the possibility of the sailor's percentage in the salvage of any wrecks. However, no wrecks came our way, and I soon tired of towing barges between Emden and Hamburg. I didn't get along well with the mate, and after a violent altercation I left the tug.

The three years of seafaring life since I left Regensburg had wrought a metamorphosis in me. I now enjoyed the roving life of a sailor. Since leaving the little *Renskea* I was no longer subject to attacks of seasickness, and had gained equally in physical stamina and self-confidence. There was no place I could call home, and no person I could go to in time of need, but I missed neither. I was ready for anything the future might hold.

Focs'le Days

A Story of my Youth

CHAPTER

1

THE GWYDYR CASTLE

THE SPRING of 1901 was not a propitious time for a sailor to find himself ashore. Hamburg, like most of the other big continental ports, was tied up by a longshoreman strike, but with the optimism of youth I was confident something would turn up. Leaving the *Blitz* with my sea bag on my shoulder I headed for the sailor's boarding house which I had left less than a month before. I had gone a few blocks, when I came across Claus, a former shipmate, who had been an A.B. (able bodied seaman) on the *Chios*. Like most of us, he had been paid off when the steamer docked in Hamburg. He had been ashore since leaving the *Chios*, and when I told him that I was going back to my old boarding house, he suggested that I change to the place where he was boarding. We had rather liked each other, and my desire for congenial companionship made me change my plans and I followed him to his boarding house.

It was a private dwelling along the St. Pauli waterfront, run by a Frau Behrens, a large, kind-hearted woman in her sixties. The basement, below street level, was used as a laundry, her principal business; the ground floor had the sleeping quarters for the sailors who boarded with her; and the rest of the house was rented out to permanent lodgers other than sailors. She was a captain's widow, and had a warm spot in her heart for all sailors. They were treated like members of her family, and we all loved her. She employed five women in the laundry. They were free and easy, and not at all above helping the boys spend their pay day. Most of the household activities were centered in the laundry room. It was also the kitchen, dining room, and served us sailors as a sitting room. In the fore part of the room, facing the street, was a big dining table, and we all ate together, the sailors, the laundresses, Frau Behrens and her little granddaughter, a pretty child of ten. I can see myself now, sitting at the table, helping her with her homework while badinage passed back and forth between the sailors and laundresses.

The strike was still hampering all port activities, and it was difficult for sailors to find ships. Most of Frau Behrens' boarders had used up all of their money, and owed board bills, but it never occurred to her to put them out. It was a rough time, and there was hardly a day when the body of a man beaten to death was not fished out of the Elbe. Sailors naturally sympathized with the strikers, but as they were not organized, their sympathies had little effect on the strike. Too, there were plenty of sailors, too many for the few ships available. The problem was chiefly in finding the ships. Beside Claus and myself, there were three other sailors, all Germans, boarding with Frau Behrens. We all got along fairly well. The atmosphere of the place was that of a home, and we all turned to, and made ourselves useful in the activities of the laundry.

I had been with Frau Behrens about a month, when my money began to get low, and I bestirred myself to find a ship, if it was possible. I went out every morning to make the rounds of the shipping offices, only to return in the evening, having had no luck. Several of the boarders owed several weeks of board, and I dreaded the idea that I should get in the same fix. Frau Behrens laughed at my scruples, she had carried sailors when they were broke before, and they had almost always come back and settled their debts.

Late one afternoon, three of us boarders were sitting at the dining table by the basement window, playing with a greasy deck of cards, by the light of a gas jet. In the steamy back of the room the laundresses were busy at their ironing boards, and Frau Behrens was at the stove getting supper. Her granddaughter was beginning to set the table, when a shadow darkened the window, and Claus descended the stone steps leading from the street. He took off his pea jacket, and warming himself by the kitchen stove gave an account of his day's activities. He had been to several shipping offices, with no luck, but he had met a former shipmate and they had had a few drinks together. On his way home he had joined a crowd watching a drowned man, one of the harbor police, being brought ashore. It was not until supper was on the table, and we had begun to eat, that he mentioned he had heard of a British sailing ship,

leaving in ballast for Cardiff, as soon as she got a crew together.

He wasn't interested at all, having had some experiences on "lime juicers," and preferred to be a bum on shore, rather than ship on one. I was intrigued, however. If there was a chance to get a berth, I would at least investigate. My money wouldn't last me more than a week, and I wasn't going to sponge on Frau Behrens. The other three sailors also showed as little enthusiasm as Claus about a "lime juicer." A British steamer perhaps, that made comparatively short trips, and could be left in any port if you didn't like her, but a British sailing ship, never. They were all hungry ships, and their voyages lasting three or four months were too long for that. They laughed at me, and filled my ears with dire predictions, when I said I was going to the British Consulate in the morning to see if I could be signed on as an A.B. While I had long ago lost my romantic notions about life at sea, I was still stirred by the sight of a big sailing ship.

The next morning I left early for the British Consulate. The anteroom was crowded with seamen of all nationalities, all looking for the kind of ship which would suit their various purposes. Then came a call for men to ship on the *Gwydyr Castle*, a British barque. There was scant response from the crowd, but five men besides myself followed the caller into an inner room, where we saw the captain of the ship, and learned the facts. We were to sign on for a three years' voyage, wages for able-bodied seamen to be three pounds, or fifteen dollars a month, and we were to board the ship immediately. Signing on for three years gave me somewhat of a shock, but I had already made up my mind to go on the ship. Amongst the five who had entered with me was one German from Hamburg, two Finns, one Swede and one Frenchman. We two Germans could not be signed on until we received permission from the German authorities, as we both would be liable for military service in a year or so. We were to report the next day, and if we had the permit, would be signed on then.

We got permits, stipulating that we would be back to enter service in the Imperial German Navy. On presenting them at the British Consulate the next day, they were not even glanced at, and we were signed on to report aboard ship the same day. I insisted on a month's advance in wages, to which the captain grudgingly agreed. Then I went back to the boarding house to break the news, pay my board bill and pack my sea bag. Claus thought I was a damned fool. It was bad enough to sail on a British ship anyway, but to sign on for three years was sheer idiocy. The others thoroughly agreed with him. However, I made the rounds, saying goodby to the women, and to Frau Behrens, who greatly embarrassed me by taking me to her ample bosom. She made me promise to come back, if I should find myself in Hamburg again.

It was late in the afternoon when I arrived at the dock where the *Gwydyr Castle* was berthed. Before going up the gangplank, I stopped to take a look at the ship which was to be my home, as it turned out, for the next two years. She was a big three-masted barque, painted slate gray, a white strip with painted black ports circling her sides. But for a double gaff to her spanker, she had nothing to distinguish her from hundreds of similar ships. Compared to the *Agustina*, the Norwegian barque, she was a giant, and I was thrilled at the sight of her tall masts and huge yards. Here finally was the ship of

my earlier dreams, and I walked up the gangplank and forward to the focs'le with a light step.

Entering the focs'le, I found I was one of the first arrivals among the new hands, and was thus able to choose the kind of bunk I wanted. I picked an upper bunk on the port side, which had a porthole to give light. It also contained a straw mattress left behind by the previous occupant. That was a windfall, as I had no mattress among my belongings. A thorough examination the next day revealed no vermin. Outside of cockroaches, the focs'le of the *Gwydyr Castle* was free of vermin of any kind, which was nothing short of a miracle, considering the various types of humanity making up her crew. We didn't mind the cockroaches.

The *Gwydyr Castle* was of Welsh ownership, though her home port was Liverpool. Besides the crew, she carried four apprentices, British lads ranging from seventeen to twenty years old. The captain, the mates and the steward were all Welsh, as were two of the crew, who had been on the ship for some time. By nightfall, all of the men newly signed on had come aboard, and everything was ready to leave the next day. There was no more shore leave that night. The next morning a tug came alongside, and towed us down the Elbe. It was a gray day, with low visibility, and little did I realize, as I watched the gray shoreline recede, that it was to be my last sight of Germany for thirty-three years, that I was leaving my homeland for good and all.

We were bound for Cardiff, Wales, there to take on a cargo of Welsh coal for Panama. As there was no Panama Canal in those days, it would mean a long voyage around Cape Horn and up the Pacific. Off Cuxhaven we put some sails on the ship. Shortly we dropped the tug's hawser and aided by the ebbing tide were standing out into Helgoland Bay. A fair northeasterly breeze carried us along, and by nightfall we were skirting the East and West Friesian Islands, reaching for the English Channel.

The deck plan of the *Gwydyr Castle* was like that of hundreds of other British sailing ships. Under the focs'le head was the windlass, the lamp and paint lockers, and the lazarette. A steel ladder led down on each side from the focs'le head to the foredeck. Then came the forehatch, with the foremast immediately behind it. Next the forward deck-house, which was made up of the focs'le, the galley, a long narrow room running the whole width of the deck-house from port to starboard, the cabin, housing the apprentices to starboard, and a cabin for the carpenter, bosun and sailmaker to port. The cook slept in the galley. The after end of the deckhouse was a big sail locker.

Following the deck-house, was the main hatch, then the mainmast, with hand pumps on either side and a big fife rail running around it, and next the afterhatch. Back of the afterhatch was a smaller deck-house, connected with the poop by a flying bridge. On top of the after deck-house was a spare binnacle, and secured in the corners of the railing were, to starboard, the barrel of salt pork, and to port, the barrel of salt beef. Behind the after deck-house was the mizzenmast, and close behind that, under the break of the poop, was a small hatch whose cover could easily be manipulated by one man. Then came the poop, with its skylights and elaborate companionway leading down into the interior of the quarter-deck. Two teakwood ladders led up to the poop from the after-deck. The quarter-deck was made up of the captain's cabin, the main salon, the chart room, quarters for the mates and steward, and the provision room. Back of the wheel was a small hatch leading down into a spare sail locker, containing mostly spare running gear. The focs'le had bunks for fourteen men in double tiers. In the fore part of the focs'le was the box containing the hardtack. On each side of the focs'le was a big locker, and likewise at the after end. In the middle stood a bogie, a small coal stove secured by guy-wires to the four corners. A kerosene lamp was the only means of illumination.

Back of the mainmast, on the main deck we carried a donkey engine, which theoretically was to help in discharging the cargo, but it was never of much use, as it always broke down, and was really only an encumbrance on deck.

The *Gwydyr Castle* carried four boats, two big life boats on top of the focs'le, cradled in their chocks on a steel frame reaching over across the deck to the rails. On the starboard quarter, similarly cradled, we carried a dinghy, and on the port quarter a gig.

The sail plan was simple. Her head sails consisted of a forestaysail and three jibs, an inner, an outer and a flying jib. Her squaresails were fore and main sails, fore and main lower and upper topsails, fore and main topgallantsails and fore and main royals. On the mizzenmast the ship carried a double spanker with two gaffs and a gaff topsail. Then besides she carried three staysails between the fore and main mast, and the same number between the main and mizzen. The ship was in good physical condition, both as to sails, rigging and running gear. Whatever economy was practiced in running the ship, was not at the expense of the ship.

We were a polygot outfit in the focs'le. Few of us could speak English, and such conversation as was carried on was in Swedish, since the Scandinavians were in the preponderance. A few days at sea had shown that there were no lame ducks among us. We were all capable seamen with sailing experience. Of the fourteen men in the focs'le, two were Welsh, one English, two German, one Frenchman, three Russian Finns, three Swedes and two Norwegians. I was the youngest amongst them, being just a few months over nineteen years old. The Frenchman was the oldest, about forty. Our ignorance of English wasn't much of a handicap, as we all knew what to do when a sailing maneuver was required. The trip over to Cardiff was more in the nature of a shakedown cruise, and we wouldn't really get to know each other well until we got started on the long trek to the Horn. We didn't know how many of us would stay with the ship either, as some were quite frank in saying that they were going to jump ship in Cardiff.

The wind stayed in the northeast and carried us along at a good clip until we were well into the English Channel. While off the Lizards the wind veered to the southwest, and we had to fight a stiff head wind before we were around Land's End and heading up into the Bristol Channel for Cardiff, where we arrived shortly, after an uneventful voyage. The trip had served both crew and officers as a sizing-up period.

The captain, a grizzled Welshman in his fifties, with a close-cropped salt-and-pepper mustache and beard, walked with a decided limp. He never addressed any of the crew, and seemed to keep himself pretty much aloof. When on the quarter-deck, he sat mostly on the skylight with his game leg stretched out on the seat. The mate was a middle-aged man with a red beard, given to blustering speech, as if to make up for his short stature, but it was all bark and no bite, and we never

took him very seriously. In bad weather it was his habit to have the men stand lookout on the poop, instead of on the focs'le head. We suspected that it wasn't so much solicitude for our welfare on his part, but a desire to have somebody to talk to. His chief topic of conversation was his brother, who was a policeman. He was full of fantastic tales of "derring do" about that brother of his, as though anxious to shine in his reflected glory. But he was a good seaman, though no driver.

The second mate was a young, dark-haired man of sallow complexion, and a nonentity as far as we were concerned. The captain made the mistake of calling him down when some of the sailors were around and consequently we had not much respect for him.

The steward, Welsh like all the officers, was a big, rather flaccid sort of man, slightly bald, with a sandy mustache. As time went on he became our especial *bête noire*, and we came to hate him thoroughly. He was responsible for the provisioning of the ship, and while undoubtedly a zealous protector of the owner's financial interests, saving pennies wherever he could, it was at the crew's expense. None of us would have shed a tear if he had been carried overboard. There was no charity in our hearts for him. The ritual of getting our lime juice at eight bells noon more often than not brought about the exchange of acrimonious remarks between him and some of us.

After arriving in Cardiff we docked at a coal pier, discharged our ballast overside into barges, and made ready to receive our cargo of coal. A couple of the hands that had shipped on in Hamburg, had had enough of the *Gwydyr Castle* and left, leaving us short-handed.

The loading of the coal commenced, and we were kept busy in the hold, shoveling and stowing the coal as it came pouring in. Every corner of the ship was covered with the all-pervading coal dust, which a persistent light drizzle turned into a nasty smudge, and the spic-and-span *Gwydyr Castle* soon assumed the look of a dirty coal barge.

We all availed ourselves of the opportunity for shore leave every evening, but there weren't many attractions in Cardiff beyond the usual waterfront pubs and dives. There was very little money amongst us, and we had been aboard the ship too short a time for the captain to give us an advance on our wages.

I had always had an instinctive admiration for everything British, their navy and merchant marine, their skill at boxing and sports, but at Cardiff doubts which had assailed me in London's Rotherhite district, and in Newcastle-on-Tyne again made me wonder if the British were so superior after all. How could any people be aware of such conditions as I saw in those big British ports, and do nothing about it? I was then unaware that such human degradation could exist anywhere.

One Sunday morning, a shipmate and I took a stroll ashore. For a change it was a sunny morning, a pleasant change from the constant drizzle and overcast skies. Reaching a district called Tiger Bay, inhabited mostly by dock workers, we came to a dead-end street, a *cul de sac*, and it presented an extraordinary spectacle. It looked like a battlefield. The sidewalks were strewn with both men and women lying around in grotesque attitudes, thoroughly vanquished in their bout with John Barleycorn. Grimy, ragged children were playing noisily in the street, oblivious of the stupefied drunks. They were merely natural obstacles in whatever game they were playing. I had seen plenty of poverty, but never poverty coupled with such degradation and squalor.

One evening I witnessed a street fight between two young women, which for tigerish ferocity and viciousness made most fisticuffs look like a pink tea. They scratched, bit, butted, and pulled hair, screaming like banshees. It was alley fighting at its worst. What made it even more disgusting, enthusiastic spectators had formed a ring around the two viragos, egging them on. When a young patrolman arrived to put a stop to the shindig, the women turned on him, and the crowd jeered. He finally subdued them with the aid of a comrade, and they were led away, blood streaming down their faces, their hair wild, and one of them with her clothes torn off, and her whole upper body, covered with scratches, exposed.

In a short while the *Gwydyr Castle* had her full cargo of coal and we left the coal dock for another pier, to get her ready for sea. No attempt was made to clean the ship while in port. That could be done when we were on the high seas, but we were waiting for two men to replace the two who had jumped ship.

We were busy on deck, making the hatches shipshape, when two men approached the gangplank and came aboard. One was a tall, gangling fellow with a scraggly mustache and carrying a clothes bundle. He was followed by a tough-looking, stocky individual in a derby, wearing a raincoat. The mate met them, and after a little palaver, the tall fellow walked forward to the focs'le and Timothy O'Sullivan became a member of the crew.

He didn't look much like a sailor to us, and the tale he told us confirmed that opinion. He had never been on a sailing ship before. All his sea experience had been confined to the stokeholds of steamers, hardly the proper apprenticeship for a man signing on as an able-bodied seaman on a squarerigger. It seemed that when he began to run up a board bill at his boarding house, his landlord had him shipped out on the first available ship, collecting an advance on his wages to cover what Tim owed him. That Tim was utterly unfit for the work on a squarerigger made no difference, and I doubt if the keeper of the boarding house would have cared, had he known, as it turned out, that in signing articles on the *Gwydyr Castle*, Tim had also signed his death warrant.

Towards evening the other man arrived. We had finished supper and were sitting around the focs'le wondering whether it was worth while to change clothes to go ashore. A persistent, fine rain was falling and the whole prospect was rather melancholy. A stream of obscene profanity preceded the new hand's appearance at the focs'le door. He was considerably the worse for wear, and looked like a thoroughly mean, tough guttersnipe, with close-set gray eyes and a moth-eaten reddish-blond beard. He was about thirty, and obviously at the end of a long debauch.

He threw his bag into the focs'le and stumbled in after it, supporting himself against the side of a bunk. His mean glance took us all in as we sat around the table by the light of the kerosene lamp. A big Finn named Ecklund was sitting next to me, and the newcomer lurched up to him.

"You are a Swede, aren't you?" the newcomer challenged.

Ecklund took the pipe out of his mouth. "No, I am a Finn, no Swede."

The drunk looked at him awhile and must have been impressed by Ecklund's size. "A Finn, eh? I like Finns,

Swedes too. I like all 'squareheads,' but I don't like the Goddamn Germans. I don't like them at all. They are all bastards."

His attention shifted to me. "What are you?"

"German."

He kept looking at me for a while, then turned away, only to come back. "You heard. I don't like the Goddamn Germans. Want to make anything of it?"

I looked him in the eye. My hackles were rising and my heart pounding, but I replied, "No!"

Nobody said anything, but we were suddenly aware that our hitherto peaceful focs'le had been invaded by a disturbing factor. The fellow went over to the remaining bunk, slung his bag into it, and produced an almost empty whiskey flask. He took the last swig, and began to volunteer some more information. He was a Liverpool Irishman, and went by the name of "Liverpool Jack." He also knew his rights and nobody was going to put anything on him. Nobody need think they could, and some day he was going to get even with that son of a bitch who had kicked him out onto a tramp sailing ship because his money had given out. He kept up his drunken monologue until the last swig of whiskey took its effect, and he tumbled fully dressed into his bunk and in a short while was dead to the world.

The rain was letting up and the skies showed signs of clearing, so we decided to spend the evening ashore. It would be the last night ashore for a long time to come. But because of the dearth of funds the fellows soon came straggling back by ones and twos. It was raining again when Ecklund and I returned to the ship around midnight. We approached the gangplank just as a horse-drawn cart jolted to a stop. The driver asked us where the *Gwydyr Castle* was. Neither Ecklund nor I knew much English, but we nodded our heads and pointed to the ship. The driver got down and dragged off a small crate. It was a little pig. Evidently the steward had bought a young pig to be delivered that day, and here it was. Would we take it off his hands? He wanted to keep the crate, so we opened it up, Ecklund took the squealing shoat in his arms, and we went up the gangplank and down onto the deck. When we reached the focs'le we sat down on the bench by the table, Ecklund with the pig in his lap. Where to put it? There was behind each steel ladder leading up to the focs'le head a steel pen, evidently for the purpose of housing a pig, but the night seemed to us too raw to put the little fellow outside without bedding.

The dim yellow light of the focs'le lamp revealed the sailors sprawled in their bunks, some fully dressed, and here and there an arm or a leg dangling over the edge of the bunk. There was a cacophony of wheezes and snores, quite drowning out the occasional squeals and grunts of the pig in Ecklund's lap. Suddenly my attention was attracted by a stentorian snort emanating from the bunk where Liverpool Jack lay sprawled in befuddled sleep. In a flash of inspiration, I suggested we put the pig in with Liverpool Jack and Ecklund enthusiastically seconded the motion. We carefully deposited the pig by his side, and though Jack stirred once or twice, he was too deep in drunken sleep to be aware of his bunk companion. The warmth soon quieted the shoat. He snuggled close to Jack and went to sleep. It wasn't long before Ecklund and I were in our bunks, and peace reigned once more in the focs'le.

Towards morning the pig became restless. It was hungry and began grunting and nosing around Liverpool Jack in search of nourishment. Jack stirred uneasily. Finally the exploratory rootings of the animal became so boisterous, it penetrated Jack's brain that something queer was going on. He roused himself onto one elbow, to find himself face to face with a pig.

He sat up with a curse and threatened to knife the dirty Goddamn so and so of a bitch responsible, if he ever found out. By this time every one had been aroused, and the general hilarity didn't soothe him either. One of the sailors got hold of the pig, before Jack in his rage could kick it out of the bunk, and took it forward to one of the pens. Thus was "Dennis," as the pig was christened, added to the roster of the ship's crew.

Dennis shared fully in our trials and tribulations. His quarters were bare of bedding, but were scrupulously clean. The ship's deck was scrubbed and washed down every morning, which included not only the pen, but Dennis himself. He always protested vigorously, but to no avail. One of us would hold him firmly, while another wielded the big deck broom on him, with perhaps unnecessary vigor. Dennis might have become a pet, but a combination of circumstances decreed otherwise. The steward had made no provision for pig food, thinking, no doubt, that there would be sufficient scraps and table leavings to keep him going. There were certainly no scraps from the focs'le, but the cook, his only friend, softened hardtack in the water our salt meat had been cooked in, and the steward brought forward the leavings from the captain's table. Our caustic remarks as he passed the focs'le on his way to the pigpen with a dish of left-over burgoo, eventually got too much for him, and he left the offerings with the cook. As the voyage progressed, we realized what a hungry ship the *Gwydyr Castle* was, and we resented the pig having burgoo, while we sat down to hardtack and black coffee.

In fine weather Dennis had the run of the ship, and was into everything, always on the quest of something to appease that aching void which must have been inside of him. No paint or tar pot left standing on deck was safe. Dennis would come snooping around, more often than not upsetting them. He had another annoying habit which didn't help endear him to us. Early each morning at the first sign of dawn, he would begin squealing and grunting for food, his squeals getting louder and louder as none was forthcoming. As his pen was close to the focs'le it invariably wakened the watch below, and many were the dire threats to make shark bait of him some dark night. Liverpool Jack, roused up one morning after a particularly strenuous midnight watch, got out of his bunk, with murder in his eye. He put on his heavy boots and went forward to the pen.

Dennis, gratified that his vociferous squeals had produced such prompt results, crowded to the barred door, his pink nose nuzzling the bars. Jack opened the door and launched a prodigious kick at Dennis' midriff, but instead of connecting with his mark, his shin bone hit the upper edge of the steel door frame. He sat down on deck, clutching his shin, and his howls of pain drowned out the pig who was squealing even louder in its frustration. Jack had to keep to his bunk for several days, nursing a shin bone he was lucky not to have broken.

One day I was busy along the port bulwarks with a pot of paint. We had chipped off all the rust spots, and I was coating the bare places with red lead. Dennis on his usual prowl, spied the pot and came over to investigate. Knowing that Dennis was about the deck, I kept the pot close to me and thought it safe. Straightening up, I turned around to load my brush, and there was Dennis.

I made a swipe at him to shoo him away, and in his precipitous flight he sideswiped the paint pot, upsetting it. There formed a large and slowly enlarging red puddle on the immaculate deck. The mate came by, and I received a bawling out for my carelessness. Dennis seemed destined to make trouble for us, and we thought of him as nothing but a nuisance. If he had given any signs of eventually turning into a fat porker, we might have been more tolerant, but he never grew, his sides were hollow and he had a regular razor back.

A few days after the episode, we were busy under the focs'le head by the paint locker. We were mixing and stirring paint when Dennis appeared around the corner of the forehatch. He eyed us warily, by this time distrustful of everybody but the steward and the cook. The sight of all those pots was too much, however, and he came nearer, when another one of my inspirations struck me.

Another fellow helped me get hold of him and while he held him, I painted Dennis in the German colors, red on his neck and shoulders, and black on his rear portions, leaving the middle white. Dennis protested vigorously, and when released tore aft along the sides of the focs'le to the main deck, where he met the mate on his way forward. By this time the commotion had brought every one on deck, the cook, the apprentices and some of the watch below.

"Catch him! Catch him!" cried the mate, and everybody tried to corner Dennis, who remained elusive. On the after part of the main deck sat the sailmaker, surrounded by clean folds of new canvas, sewing on a new jib. Dennis, getting more frantic by the minute, eluded the outstretched hands of the men stationed by the mainmast and made a bee line for the snowy heaps of canvas. The sailmaker jumped up, shouting maledictions at things in general and the pig in particular. At last Dennis was cornered among the now red-and-black-spotted canvas.

The captain and the mate were furious, not to mention the old sailmaker. The mate came forward to the paint locker, reading the riot act, but, though he may have had his suspicions, he never found out just who was responsible. Dennis was brought forward and cleaned with turpentine—a cure which for Dennis was worse than the disease.

Dennis met his death off Cape Horn. Life off the Horn was miserable enough for us humans, but we could at least get into the shelter of the focs'le and into our bunks. Dennis, in his steel pen, was completely exposed to the weather and his pen was often half awash with the green water the ship took over both sides with great abandon. There came a day when all hell broke loose, and the *Gwydyr Castle* wallowed, seemingly as much under water as above it.

The cook, becoming aware of the pig's plight, decided to get it out of its pen and put it temporarily in the galley. He worked his way forward, got Dennis, and holding him in his arms, began carefully to work his way aft again towards the galley door. Dennis was just big enough to make an uncomfortable armful, as the cook had to use one hand to support himself on the wildly heaving deck. Just as he neared the galley, the ship heeled over hard, scooping up tons of green water over her port bulwarks. The cook clung frantically to the guard rail running along the side of the deck-house, but Dennis was torn from his weakened grasp, and disappeared in a welter of foamy green water. Our last glimpse of Dennis was of him riding atop a gray comber rolling away to leeward.

The morning after the advent of Dennis and Liverpool Jack on board everybody was called on deck after breakfast to get the ship ready for departure. The skies had cleared during the night, and gold and pink clouds covered the eastern sky. A tug came alongside, and at high tide we left Cardiff. Out in the Bristol Channel we swarmed up the rigging, loosening sails, and getting the ship gradually under canvas. The tug cast off and turned about, giving us a farewell toot. The coast of Wales got dimmer and dimmer, and by the time the royals had been set, we had seen the last sign of land for many weary months to come.

CHAPTER
2

CARDIFF TO CAPE HORN

THE GWYDYR CASTLE, favored by a fair wind, was dipping into a westerly swell and the whole crew turned to, to clean the ship. Our stay in Cardiff had made the ship a sorry sight. Everything on deck was covered with a film of coal dust which had pervaded even the interior of the focs'le and the cabin. It took us several days before the ship emerged her normal spic-and-span self. Watches were not set until eight o'clock that evening. At that time all hands went aft to the break of the poop where the mates would choose the members of their respective watches. The first mate would pick a man, then the second mate had his choice, and so they alternated until the crew was evenly divided into a port and a starboard watch.

I was chosen for the mate's port-watch and was glad to see that Fatty Ecklund also belonged to my watch, and even more glad when the second mate chose Liverpool Jack for his watch. I had an instinctive feeling that sooner or later it would come to a showdown between Liverpool Jack and me. The chances for that were greatly reduced when we were not in the same watch. While my knowledge of English was still rudimentary, I spoke Swedish quite fluently and as most members of my watch were Scandinavians or Finns, I felt more at home with them.

Fatty Ecklund was a big raw-boned Finn, who had lost an eye in an accident at sea. Like most Finns he was a very good sailor and as strong as an ox, a good man to be next to on a yard. Like everybody else, he shortly acquired a nickname. He became "Fatty" not because he was pudgy, but because of his size. He was good-natured and always even-tempered. He became my only real pal. Another of the Finns was called "the little Finn," largely because of his contrast to the huge Ecklund. Though small of stature, he was a very good hand, but rather belligerent in speech and manner, and quick to take offense. He was an excellent checker player, and while his opposition may not have been firstclass we never succeeded in winning a game from him during the two years we were shipmates. The third Finn was a quiet fellow, rather nondescript and just one of the hands, though a good sailor.

There were five British sailors, if Tim Sullivan could be classed as a sailor. Two of them were Welshmen. The first was a young fellow named William Williams who had the bunk next to me. We thought that he came from the captain's home town, but were not sure, as he was very uncommunicative about his personal affairs. He was a tall, dark-haired, loosely-put-together chap and was not the sort of drifter most deep-water sailors were. His clothes and outfit were better, and he was one of the very few of us who received mail from home in the various ports. The second Welshman had the bunk below me. He was a small sandy-haired man with a big mustache, all out of proportion to the rest of him. He was an indifferent sailor but a great talker, though no one ever took him seriously. He didn't know his parents, and had run away to sea at the age of thirteen, stowing himself away in a lifeboat aboard a sailing ship. Fortunately, the captain, before whom he was brought when discovered, was a kindly man with a sense of humor. To put the lad in the focs'le was out of the question, and he made the voyage to Australia and back home again as cabin boy. He had never had such a good time before or since.

The third of the British contingent was an Englishman. He remained a mystery to us right up to the time we parted company in New York two years later. A medium-sized man with a scrubby mustache, he somehow didn't seem to belong in a focs'le. He always managed to have money and never had to coax a dollar or a few shillings out of the captain when in port. He never joined any of us when on shore leave and just before leaving a port he stocked up with all sorts of delicacies, cigars, candy, chocolate bars, condensed milk and the like, which he stored in his sea chest and secreted around his bunk. We were aware of his squirrel habits, and only waited for his first turn at the wheel, when he would be absent for two hours, to ransack his bunk. A man's bunk was usually inviolate, but there

was something about the man and his habits that rubbed us the wrong way. We called him "Birmingham." He must have been well educated because at times during a dog-watch he would get up on the forehatch and, much to our astonishment, recite poetry, sonorous verses from Milton and Shakespeare. It certainly came under the heading of casting pearls before swine. He was familiar with all forms of practical seamanship, though he always gave us the impression that he didn't quite pull his weight.

Then there was "Liverpool Jack" who, but for his smallish size, would have been a real bully. He had reddish hair and a scraggly beard of the same hue. He was a Liverpool Irishman who had been either a foundling or an orphan very early in life, and told us that he had been brought up on one of the maritime school ships lying in the Mersey. He was a tough, pugnacious customer, always looking for trouble, always talking about his rights, the perfect "sea lawyer." He would have liked nothing better than to keep us "squareheads" in our place, and resented it that we were not at all impressed with his presumption. He was, however, a good sailor, and that, after all, was the standard by which men were judged in the focs'le.

The last of the Britishers was Tim Sullivan, the coal passer. He was, of course, no sailor and didn't know one rope from another, couldn't steer and was only fit to stand lookout. He was a tall, sandy-haired chap, giving the impression of being rather badly put together, and was considered so much excess baggage by the rest of us. We all wondered how he would do when the going got rough.

Besides myself, there was another German lad, about my age. His home was in Hamburg and, like

Williams, the Welshman, he was a different type from the rest of us. He had served his apprenticeship on a big nitrate carrier running between Hamburg and Iquique, Chile, and, despite his youth, knew more seamanship than any other man in the focs'le. He had a definite home background in Hamburg and had signed on the *Gwydyr Castle* for the experience, and to learn the English language. Though I was the only other German aboard, we never became very intimate.

I was then nineteen years of age and had been to sea for three years. From the puny boy, who in the orphan asylum was thought to have weak lungs, I had developed into a husky lad, weighing one hundred and fifty pounds. I was very strong and muscular and quick on my feet. I still had a lot to learn about seamanship, but at tailing onto a rope or fighting a sail on the yard I was as good as any of them. My unhappy childhood was by this time merely a bad dream, and I had gotten over my prolonged spells of moodiness and spiritual depression. Life was not a bed of roses, but I enjoyed my freedom and did a man's work, which bolstered my self-confidence. I had no home and was a drifter on the seven seas. The dreams I had had as a child of becoming an artist, I had buried and I just drifted along with the tide, not thinking of what the future might hold in store for me. I was a good sailor and got along well with my shipmates. I had a sense of the dramatic and extracted every ounce of esthetic enjoyment out of the life aboard ship, seeing beauty and grandeur, even under conditions when physical existence was hazardous and uncomfortable. They nicknamed me "Bismarck," and I had a suspicion that the name was given me for not altogether complimentary reasons.

The rest of the crew were more or less nondescript.

At least they left no particular impression on me.

The four apprentices, who had quarters of their own and really belonged to the afterguard, were quite a different type from the focs'le gang. They were all English, and were destined to become officers in the British Merchant Marine. They ranged in age from sixteen to nineteen. As they had their own quarters and mess, they mixed very little with the crew.

The boatswain was a middle-aged Welshman, a quiet and easy-going man. The carpenter was a Russian from Esthonia, who kept very much to himself, quite unlike the old sailmaker, who loved to mix with the crew in the dog-watches. He was an old fellow who might have been anything from sixty to seventy-five years of age. We all thought he was over seventy. He was as grand an old seadog as ever sailed the seven seas, a huge man, with a bald pate encircled by a fringe of gray hair, a massive chest, and enormous gnarled hands. He was a Swede and had served in the United States Navy during the Civil War. He had been all over the world on ships of all nationalities, had a smattering of half a dozen different languages and was a mine of information about everything pertaining to ships and the sea, and often would join us in the dog-watch, sit on the forehatch and hold us spellbound with tales of his adventures. He loved especially to brag about his feminine conquests, and needed little urging to elaborate on his amatory adventures in all the big ports of the world. We all liked and respected him and especially when the men were called aloft to take in a mainsail or a foresail and found old "Sails" amongst them. The topsail and gallant yards were a little too much for him.

The cook was a Negro from the Argentine, a hot-tempered black man with bloodshot eyes. He had the most extraordinary hair I have ever seen on a human being. It was grayish black, about three inches in length and stood straight out from his scalp. His head seemed surrounded by a halo of smudge. Relations between the crew and the cook were rather strained. We blamed the cook for a lot of things of which he was really innocent. Eventually we came to realize that it was not the cook but the steward who was responsible for the skimpiness and bad quality of the food served up to us. The cook didn't mix with anybody, and as he bunked in the galley, he rarely came on deck, unless it was to feed Dennis, the pig.

Watches were four hours on deck, and four hours below. The afternoon watch from four P.M. to eight P.M. was divided into two watches called dog-watches. Their main purpose was to alternate the night watches so that the port-watch would have two night watches one night and the starboard-watch would have them the next night. Nobody went below during the dog-watches, especially in fine weather, and no work was required excepting such handling of the sails as might be needed. It was our recreation period.

After the watches had been set, we immediately fell into the regular ship's routine. Leaving Bristol Channel behind we continued to enjoy fair weather with variable winds, until we struck the northeast Trades. Then the *Gwydyr Castle* bowled along under a fair wind over a blue sea. By this time every vestige of the filth collected in Cardiff had been removed. The deck had been holy-stoned and all the paintwork cleaned.

The fresh meat taken on in Cardiff had been used up long ago. The *Gwydyr Castle* had no refrigeration and the amount of fresh provisions she could carry was extremely limited. The potatoes were giving out too. We weren't long in discovering that the owners of the ship were very parsimonious and that they had in the steward a loyal employee who saw eye to eye with them.

The British Board of Trade had decreed the absolute minimum of food a seaman was entitled to. We received that minimum and not an ounce more. British sailing ships were notorious amongst sailors all over the world for their scanty, monotonous fare. Why the greatest seafaring nation in the world should have had such a policy, I could never understand, unless the profit instinct was so ingrained in its traders that penny pinching had become a virtue. Scandinavian ships, especially the Norwegians, French, German and American ships provided good food in variety and plenty of it. It was a rare thing to find a British sailing ship with an all-British crew. Their crews were mostly the sweepings of the seven seas, in contrast with the German and Scandinavian ships, invariably manned by their own nationals.

On the *Gwydyr Castle* our weekly menu ran thus: Mondays, salt beef and beans; Tuesdays, salt pork and peas; Wednesdays, again salt beef and beans; on Thursdays it was "canned Willie" (Australian canned mutton) and soft bread which went by the name of "Rootie"; Fridays, salt pork and peas; Saturdays, salt beef and beans; and Sunday's meal was a duplicate of Thursday's. During our two years' voyage that routine never varied, excepting during our stay in port, when we received fresh meat and potatoes if available. We could tell eight months ahead just what meal would come to the table on any given date. We never saw a fresh vegetable of any kind with the exception of the occasional potatoes and, in some ports, yams. The only thing provided for unlimited consumption was hardtack, which was kept in a large box along the forward bulkhead of the focs'le. The hardtack was a grayish-yellow color, about four inches square and three-quarters of an inch thick.

Breakfast came at eight A.M., when one watch relieved the other, and was partaken of by both watches. It consisted of a horrible brew, misnamed coffee, and hardtack. Supper was at six P.M. in the dog-watch, and consisted of an equally nasty brew supposed to be tea, and hardtack. If the coffee and the tea were not particularly palatable, they at least served the purpose of making the hardtack edible. In its natural state it was as hard as cement, and in the course of time became thoroughly infested with weevils. We would pound the hardtack into pieces and drop them into our pannikins of hot tea or coffee. In a minute or so the weevils would rise to the surface to be skimmed off. This preliminary operation finished, we would consume our breakfast or supper, as the case might be.

Each man also received a half pound of sugar, a half pound of margarine and a half pound of marmalade per week. To preserve our margarine in tropical weather, we mixed it with the marmalade, and a gooey, unpalatable mess it became towards the end of the week. To prevent the outbreak of scurvy aboard their ships, the British law required that each man be furnished a daily ration of lime juice. At eight bells noon each day we all went aft to where the steward was stationed by the afterhatch with a pail of lime juice, and had our pannikins filled. This ritual was the origin of the term

"Limejuicer," by which British ships were known all over the world.

The old sailmaker showed us how to vary our diet by making a concoction called "dandyfunk." We filled a small canvas bag with hardtack and pounded it into cracker dust with a serving mallet. As there was no way to extract the weevils from the hardtack in its dry state, they were simply pounded into the dust. Then, if the cook was on comparatively good terms with us, he would mix the cracker dust with the liquid in which the salt beef or pork had been cooked, and some molasses, and bake it for us. The resulting concoction was almost as hard as the original hardtack, but at least it was a variation.

Later, while in the equatorial region, we caught boobies, a species of sea bird. At sundown they would light on the yards and made no attempt to fly away when we went up after them. We picked them off like tame chickens and attempted to use them for a "meat pie," but the result had such a rank, fishy taste that we never repeated the experiment.

Fresh water was carried in a big tank amidships down in the hold, and was carefully rationed. Our daily ration of water was deposited in a four-gallon tank in the focs'le, and was used only for drinking purposes. Fresh water for washing was out of the question. We washed our clothes in salt water from over the side and could get salt-water soap for that purpose from the slop chest. The slop chest was a sort of ship's commissary where we could get plug tobacco, salt-water soap, sheath knives, rubber boots, oilskins and a few articles of clothing, against our wages. It was run by the steward, and also served to siphon off a part of our scanty wages. The plug tobacco was of a rectangular shape. We cut it into small, geometrically exact squares, which served amongst us as a medium of exchange, mostly in games of poker or Black Jack. The slop chest was really a neccessary institution aboard ship, though we suspected the steward of making a good profit on each transaction. That may have been unfair, as we suspected the steward at all times, but with some justice, as subsequent events proved.

As far as our experience went, there was only one type of medicine used aboard the *Gwydyr Castle*, and that was "Black Draught." It was a mixture of sulphur and molasses, and was given impartially for an attack of malaria, carbuncles or a sprained leg.

The only reading matter I saw was a dog-eared, paper copy of *Nicholas Nickleby*. I found it in my bunk when I first boarded the ship in Hamburg. I read and reread it at least a dozen times and it was my guide to the English language. It always gave me a great thrill when I came to the end of the book, where the boys turn on the master of Dotheboys Hall and give him a sound beating. There may have been books in the cabin, but if so we had no access to them.

Each watch would appoint a man by turns to act as "Peggy" for a week. "Peggy" had to get the grub from the galley and serve it up. He had to cut the chunk of salt beef or pork into as equal portions as possible. As he had to take the last piece in the dishpan, it was pure self-interest that made him very careful to cut the meat into as equal portions as possible. He also had to clean up after meals, and see to it that the focs'le was kept clean, the kerosene lamp filled, and the coal stove kept going in cold weather. Every morning at eight bells (eight A.M.) he had to go aft to the flying bridge where the steward would weigh out the piece of salt meat for that day's meal, each determined that correct weight should be given, "Peggy" to see that it wouldn't be an ounce underweight, and the steward to see to it that it wouldn't be a fraction of an ounce over the weight. On many sailing ships there was a slide opening between the focs'le and the galley through which the food was passed directly, but we had no such arrangement on the *Gwydyr Castle*, and later, off Cape Horn, bringing the food along the deck was often a hazardous duty.

Life aboard the ship had become definitely routine and existence reduced to the absolute essentials, the watch on deck, the watch below, the turn at the wheel, the turn at lookout, the midday meal, and the bunk. After the ship was thoroughly cleaned, we were busy overhauling all running and standing gear. The northeast trade winds carried us along without a break so that the sails and their braces needed hardly any attention.

We had plenty of chance to size each other up and we all got along fairly well in the focs'le. There was a tendency amongst some of our British shipmates to impress upon us the fact that the *Gwydyr Castle* was a British ship and that we non-Britishers were foreigners. At first we ignored it, but when Tim Sullivan began to refer to some of us as "squareheads," we rather resented it. None of us non-Britishers had sufficient command of the English language to talk back with appropriate sarcasm, but we knew that sooner or later the situation would come to a head. Just how soon none of us realized.

It started on a beautiful moonlight night. My watch, the port-watch, was on deck. A steady northeast wind was blowing, and there wasn't the remotest chance that we would be called upon for a sail maneuver. The watch below had a poker game going, with plug tobacco as chips. The fellows of the deck-watch, one by one, slipped into the focs'le to watch the game. I even slipped into my bunk, from which vantage point I had a good view of what went on around the table. All of a sudden, the first mate appeared at the focs'le door. Wise to the way of sailors he had left the poop and meandered forward along the main deck. When he didn't encounter a single man of his watch, he made tracks for the focs'le and found his deck-watch absorbed in watching the game. He blew up, and, finding me sprawled out in my bunk, I became the special target for his wrath. We beat it on deck as fast as we could, followed by the laughter and jeers of the watch below. At eight bells midnight, we roused the watch below, and when they came on deck to relieve us, Tim kept the incident alive by more jeering and sarcastic remarks. He seemed to direct the remarks to me especially. My inability to answer him in kind enraged me, and suddenly, without warning, I swung at him. He swung back at me and we tangled. Before we could harm each other we were separated. Liverpool Jack assumed the role of umpire, and everybody agreed with him when he thought it was too dark to have a fight right then and there. But it called for a fight, and the next day's dog-watch was set as the time to have it out.

When I went below my rage evaporated as quickly as it had risen, and the reaction set in. I had no grudge against Tim. True enough, our opinion of him as a sailor was very low, but nobody disliked him, and the occasional flaunting of his British nationality more amused than angered us. I didn't want to fight Tim at all, but to get out of it I had to humble myself and apologize since I had struck the first blow, and that would make me lose caste amongst my shipmates. I was more afraid of that than being licked. Boxing seemed to me then a special British accomplishment and I fully expected to take a humiliating beating. I was under tension all day and Liverpool's whispered conversations with Tim, and his dire predictions, only added to my state of apprehension.

That afternoon in the dog-watch the sailors gathered on the forward deck by the focs'lehead. Liverpool Jack assumed the role of master of ceremonies and referee. We had no gloves and the fight was to be with bare fists. There were no rounds, but when a man was down, the other fellow couldn't hit him. If one of us couldn't get up by the count of ten, the other would be the winner. Tim and I faced each other, and the first thing I knew, Tim landed squarely on my nose bringing blood, and at the same time, tears to my eyes. Before I had a chance to recover he landed another blow on the same spot. I stepped back out of range amidst the derisive laughter of the onlookers, with Liverpool Jack especially vociferous, yelling to Tim to go on and "knock my block off." It all combined to throw me in a rage and I tore into Tim with both arms flailing. If I was hit, I was unconscious of it. All I wanted was to beat down my tormentor. Suddenly, after a wild mix-up, Tim was down on deck and such was my blind rage that I forgot all about our agreement, that the man down couldn't be hit. I went for Tim, but was stopped by Liverpool Jack and one of the Norwegians.

Tim was down on all fours and was bleeding from a cut under his eye. When he rose I went right at him again, and shortly he went down once more, with the

sailors forming the ring, howling like dervishes. Tim was just getting to his feet again when the mate, attracted by the noise, appeared around the corner of the focs'le and put a stop to the fight. I was bleeding from the nose and mouth, and Tim had both eyes swollen and bled from a cut across the nose. The reaction was too much for me. I went over to the scuppers and became violently nauseated. My right hand felt numb and began to swell. I had sprained it during the shindig with my wild hitting. After we had both recovered I went over to Tim and offered to shake hands, which he accepted, and that was the end of it.

The fight did serve one purpose in that it cleared the atmosphere in the focs'le. It served notice that we might be foreigners or "squareheads" on a British ship, but that we weren't going to be anybody's door mat.

For a couple of days after the fight life ran along in the same monotonous groove. Then tragedy struck the ship. The spell of fine weather and easy sailing were utilized for overhauling every bit of running gear, from the royal yard down, not only running gear but foot-ropes, shrouds and stays, in preparation for the tough times that were bound to come off Cape Horn. Every deck-watch went aloft, putting on chafing gear, where needed, tarring, greasing and serving and replacing weakened ratlines. It was the sort of work sailors liked the best.

One beautiful morning my watch had been relieved at eight bells (eight A.M.) and after our breakfast of coffee and hardtack, I went on deck to wash some clothes. It was a perfect day, the ship moving along before a gentle breeze, under a cloudless sky. I went to the rail and dipped up a bucket of water from over the side. Putting it down on deck and straightening up, I cast a casual glance aft, to be frozen in my tracks.

A shadowy form streaked down along the starboard main rigging. The deck-house shut off my view of the main deck to starboard, but there was a sickening thud. It happened so quickly, I couldn't find my voice for a few seconds. Then I rushed to the focs'le door and shouted, "Man overboard!" Everybody piled out on deck and ran aft. The first mate was already at the scene of the accident, while the second mate had pushed the helmsman aside and was putting the helm down hard to throw the ship up into the wind. The captain came on deck to take charge, first throwing a life preserver over the poop rail. The little Finn came scurrying down the ratlines from the royal yard where he and Tim had been working. We all stood by the rail, gazing at the spattered brains and blood where Tim's head had struck before he dropped over the side. The little Finn didn't know how it had happened. Both he and Tim had been up on the royal yard, the Finn working along the starboard yard arm and Tim amidships. He had heard a yell and looking around saw Tim catapulting down the rigging. He had either lost his footing or taken hold of a rope which wasn't belayed on deck.

There was no sign of Tim in the waters around the ship, and after the bloody evidence on the starboard rail, it was unlikely that he was alive. However, as a matter of form, rather than from any hope of finding him, we put the gig over. When it hit the water, we found that the bottom plug was missing and the water came pouring in through the hole. I took off my tam-o'-shanter and stuffed it in, while the mate went to search for the plug. After about five minutes he found it

in the bottom drawer of his bureau in his cabin. There were four of us and the bosun in the boat when we pulled away from the ship. We made a wide circle and picked up the life preserver, but there was no sign of Tim.

The tragedy cast a pall over the ship. It had come so literally like a bolt from the blue. It seemed almost impossible that such a thing could happen under the ideal condition of sea and weather. But Tim had had no sailing-ship experience and the royal yard was a pretty risky place for an inexperienced hand.

I felt worse than any one on board. Tim still carried the marks of our fight when he catapulted to his death, and I had the uneasy feeling that I had some indirect responsibility in the matter. When I discussed it with Fatty Ecklund, he told me to forget it. Tim had signed on as an able-bodied seaman, and had to do the work of one. If he was inexperienced, it wasn't my fault, and if the second mate hadn't sent him up to the royal yard, he would be alive at that minute. But I would have given anything if Tim and I hadn't fought that bloody battle a few days before. I wanted to do something to make amends and salve my uneasy conscience, so I decided to make a memorial to Tim. I spoke to the mate about it and he gave me a piece of stiff white paper. I spent a week lettering and decorating. The result read:

IN MEMORIAM
TIMOTHY O'SULLIVAN
born in Cork
DIED AT SEA
JUNE 10, 1901
REQUIESCAT IN PACE

The carpenter made a frame for it, and we hung it in the focs'le. However, most of the sailors had seen death strike a shipmate suddenly and unexpectedly at some time or another. It was one of the hazards of a sailor's life aboard a sailing ship, and the memory of Tim and his tragic death was short-lived.

We ran out of the northeast trades and into waters teeming with fish of all kinds. The watch below always had a man or two out on the jib-boom, dabbing a line for a dolphin or bonito. Bonitos became a very welcome addition to our monotonous fare, aside from the fact that catching them was a great sport, even if hard on the hands. It always took two men to land one. One man sat athwart the jib-boom, letting the wind carry the line out to leeward. The bait was nothing but a white rag, which the wind kept bobbing and dancing on top of the water. It was a thrilling sight to see a big bonito break water and launch itself into the air after the elusive bait. To bring the hooked fish in under the jib-boom and then haul it up was the hardest kind of work. How hard can best be appreciated by any one who has hooked onto a bonito while sitting in a comfortable chair in the stern of a cabin cruiser and brought the fish alongside with good fishing tackle. When the bonito was lifted out of the water, hand over hand, he became a blur of frenzied struggle. The other man was ready with a burlap bag to "net" the fish.

Occasionally we would hook onto a dolphin, the swiftest member of the finny tribe, and just before his death, when he changes to all colors of the rainbow, one of the most beautiful. We never used the dolphins for food, since the old sailmaker, whom we considered an oracle in such matters, said that they were poisonous.

The biggest fish we landed by hand line was an albacore. I hooked onto him in calm weather right under the bow of the ship. He weighed twenty-two pounds. As we approached the equatorial latitudes we sighted more and more marine life, huge sea turtles, sharks, sawfish, giant rays, bonitos, dolphins, albacore, skipjacks and flying fish. The latter occasionally landed on deck, attracted by the running lights of the ship. A huge whale kept the ship company once for two days and two nights. He came as close as a stones throw at times, close enough so that we could see the barnacles and marine growth encrusting his tough old hide. It would have been more considerate of the old mossback if he had kept astern or to leeward of the ship, but he would appear to windward, to spout and blow, and his foul breath polluted the air all around the ship.

As we approached the region of the doldrums preparations were made to change all sails from heavy to light weather canvas. We might be delayed in the doldrums from one to three weeks, and with the ship rolling in the oily swell, the constant slatting and banging of the sails against the masts and rigging, would wreak havoc with our good canvas. We spent several days changing it, and it was then that sharks made their appearance. The sight of a triangular black fin cleaving the surface of water had something ominous about it. It looked even more ominous while we were aloft, when we looked down into the blue depths and saw sharks circling the ship. We hated the very sight of them, and no sooner was the deck-watch relieved, than we made preparations to catch them.

The mate gave us the big shark hook, and prevailed upon the steward to let us have a chunk of salt pork.

The hook was fastened to a two-foot length of chain, and that in turn to strong manila rope. The bait would attract one of the big marauders, and turning his white belly up, he would grab it. After he had swallowed the bait, his and our struggle commenced. He would thrash around, lashing the water into foam, while we fastened a turn of the rope around a belaying pin. To get the monster on deck a running bowline was rigged around the line fast to the shark. The fellows would then haul on the rope, lifting the shark out of the water, whereupon the running bowline was passed down over the shark's head until the bight of the rope reached the small of his tail. Then it was hauled taut and the fish was secured at both ends. Then we hauled the shark aboard, where he thrashed violently, making every one take care to avoid the flailing tail. The bowline fastened to the tail was belayed, the rope fastened to the hook taken to a capstan and the hook was pulled out of his gullet by main force. It was all a rather cruel and messy performance, but sailors always have had an instinctive dread of sharks and the men were completely callous about it. It never occurred to us that shark meat might be edible, for which I suppose our dread of them was responsible, but we used the skin for abrasive purposes and once, when we caught a big brute, almost ten feet in length, one of the sailors cut out the jaw with its wicked triangular teeth to eventually use it as a frame for a small ship's model. To bleach the bone and rid it of its adhering flesh and gristle, he towed it over the side for almost three weeks. By that time the friction of the water had made it clean as a hound's tooth. Sometimes sailors followed the same process with the shark's spine, which was then made into a walking cane.

We hated the doldrums. The heat was clammy and oppressive and day after day the *Gwydyr Castle* wallowed in the oily glassy swell, her sails slatting and banging.

Our deck-watches were spent mostly in chipping rust and touching up the paintwork. I was detailed one day to paint the figurehead of the ship, and went somewhat beyond my instructions when I beautified the regal lady with carmine lips and cheeks. We were constantly called to trim the yards, clew up the sails and then set them again. A catspaw would appear off the horizon carrying the promise of a breeze and we would trim the sails to meet it, only to have the zephyr die out before reaching the ship. Then the same thing would happen from another quarter, with the same disappointment.

Every one was infected with a feeling of frustration, and the atmosphere in the focs'le was quarrelsome. The fellows snarled at each other, and the slightest provocation started a row, often ending in fisticuffs.

There were intervals when the heavens opened and showered their blessing down on us. One day the skies darkened, and the horizon was blotted out by a wall of rain. It was a perfect deluge. We plugged all the scupper holes and in a short time the deck was flooded inches deep with delicious rainwater. We all stripped to the skin and everything washable was brought out on deck, which soon resembled a busy laundry. None of us had felt fresh water on our faces, let alone our bodies, since we had left Cardiff, and what a luxury a real necessity can become! Personal hygiene simply had no place on a windjammer. The downpour also served to replenish our supply of fresh water in the tank down in the hold.

And so we drifted along in the doldrums, gradually edging our way south, until one morning at eight bells we were called out to find the ship heeling slightly and the welcome sound of rippling water along the bow. A breeze had sprung up during the night, and this time it was no false alarm. It carried us steadily south, leaving the doldrums behind. The light sails were unbent and replaced by storm canvas. By the time the sails were replaced, the ship picked up the southeast trades and with a fair, fresh wind the *Gwydyr Castle* made rapid progress southward.

THE DOLDRUMS

CHAPTER
3

CAPE HORN

THE SOUTHEAST trade winds carried us along at a good clip and we were approaching the Southern Forties, a treacherous region, swept by frequent southwesterly gales. Reaching the waters off River Plate we had our first demonstration of what Cape Horn had in store for us. I relieved Fatty Ecklund at the wheel. He gave me the course and said the mate had told him the barometer was falling, and they expected a blow before very long. Shortly the mate came over to the binnacle to see that I was steering the right course and then volunteered the same information to me. He was a sociable soul and loved to talk. He was not a driver and had nothing of the "bucco" about him. He must have known that the crew wasn't any too well treated in the matter of food, but as one of the ship's officers he never voiced an opinion on that subject to us. The temperature began to fall and an ominous haze was beginning to obscure the southwestern horizon. The deck-watch was sent aloft to take in the royals. The outer jib and gaff topsail were hauled down and furled. The wind increased by the minute and the dark clouds to the west were torn by lightning. Then both watches were sent aloft to take in the mainsail and put reefs in the upper topsails. Soon the ship

was in the grip of a *pampero* and the *Gwydyr Castle* began to labor hard in the rapidly rising sea. Life lines were stretched fore and aft. The gale increased steadily and at eight bells midnight both watches went aloft to take in the foresail and both upper topsails. Then the ship was hove to under lower topsails and the forestaysail. There was no let-up to the force of the wind and when my watch came on deck at eight bells (eight A.M.) a wild sea was raging. It was the *Gwydyr Castle's* first real test, and what she showed us was not reassuring.

She was a deeply laden ship and proved very sluggish in a heavy sea, taking green water both to windward and leeward impartially. I clawed my way aft along the lifeline to relieve the man at the wheel, and standing there, a magnificent spectacle was spread out before me. The skies were clearing and big patches of blue appeared amongst the windtorn clouds. The ship would pitch down into a deep-blue valley of water, with a mountainous wall of water obliterating the horizon to windward, then she would laboriously rise to the crest of the wave, revealing a panorama of rhythmic indigo hills and valleys, marbled with foamy patterns. The sheer beauty of the scene was almost intoxicating. As if to welcome us on our approach to that watery hell, off

Cape Horn an albatross appeared, gliding and swooping, in and out of the troughs of the waves, then soaring on high, hovering motionless, the very poetry of effortless motion. Later in the afternoon the wind began to moderate and as the barometer was slowly rising the captain had the foresail shaken out and sheeted home, then we set the reefed upper topsails again. The ship was put back on her course. By next morning the blow was over and we put the *Gwydyr Castle* back under full sail again, heading for the Falkland Islands.

We sailed south under moderate winds and overcast skies. Then thick weather set in as we approached the vicinity of the Falklands. For almost a week the captain had been unable to take an observation and the lead was brought aft and heaved every quarter of an hour. Then the fog evaporated and an intermittent sun enabled the captain to take observations and orient himself. Albatrosses appeared quite frequently now and swarms of cape pigeons flocked around the ship like a reception committee. The weather turned colder by the hour. Leaving the doldrums of the equatorial region we had been sailing steadily south towards the south Atlantic winter. We set up the bogie in the focs'le, a small coal stove secured by four guywires to screw eyes in the deck, and kept going by whoever happened to be "Peggy."

One morning I was at the wheel, warmly enough dressed but still chattering with the cold. The mate noticed it and stopped by the binnacle.

"What's the matter, Bismarck, are you sick?"

"I'm cold," I replied. "Could one of the fellows relieve me for a minute, so I can put on my oilskins?"

He looked at me and grinned.

"Go ahead! I'll take the wheel long enough for that. And while you're at it you might put on some boots and socks." No wonder I felt cold. Going barefoot was as natural to me as breathing, and I had forgotten my feet as I gradually put on warmer clothing, but I discovered then that no amount of warm clothing would keep you comfortable in cold weather if the feet were either wet or cold.

The ship approached the 50° latitude South and, having left the Falkland Islands behind us, our course was shifted more westerly every day. Cape Horn is on the extreme tip of South America. The prevailing winds are westerly and to cross the Cape and get around into the Pacific means bucking constant head winds. Gales would be a better word, especially during the winter months. We reached the Cape Horn region towards the end of July, midwinter in the Southern Hemisphere. After two hours lookout on the focs'lehead or two hours at the wheel, exposed to the biting cold wind, it was a real comfort to step into the focs'le and squat by the red-hot bogie for a few minutes before joining the rest of the watch huddled under the focs'lehead, sheltered somewhat from the wind.

But we weren't to enjoy its warmth-giving blessing very long. It began to blow and soon the *Gwydyr Castle* struggled in a full westerly gale. An enormous sea rose and the ship rolled and pitched fearfully. The starboard-watch had gone below, weary, tired and wet when the ship rolled over to leeward, burying her bulwark and inviting the whole South Atlantic aboard. Slowly she righted herself to repeat the process to windward, shifting the weight of water which filled her deck from the focs'lehead to the poop. In some way the

focs'ledoor had come open, and water poured into the focs'le. While the watch below was struggling to close the door, a sea chest was torn loose from its lashings and, in washing back and forth, banged into the guy-wires of the bogie, loosening them. Before the guy-wires could be secured, the ship took another deep roll to the leeward, throwing the bogie with it and loosening the remaining wires, so that the sea chest and the bogie were playing tag in the flooded focs'le. The door of the bogie flew open, scattering red-hot coals and filling the focs'le with reek and steam. Some of the coals landed in a lower bunk, setting the straw mattress on fire. Finally the chest and the bogie were secured and the fire put out. Several of the sailors had received burns and abrasions and most were frightened enough to decide to do without the stove from then on, at least while off the Horn.

Thinking back on the two nightmarish months it took the *Gwydyr Castle* to get around Cape Horn, I often wonder how we survived at all. It was a succession of westerly gales, the ship hove to half the time under two lower topsails, making two feet south or north to every foot west; blizzards when we couldn't see thirty yards beyond the ship and huge gray seas would loom up to windward like nebulous monsters; sleet storms when rigging and footropes became coated with ice, when coiled and belayed ropes were solid blocks of ice to be pounded apart and when sails were stiff as boards and as unmanageable. The *Gwydyr Castle* now justified all our fears during the *pampero* off River Plate. Deeply laden as she was and with the cargo badly stowed, she lay in the water like a dead weight and showed little buoyancy. The deck was never free of water, and the men went to their watch below soaked through. Before going on deck we tied rope yarn around the sleeves at the wrists and the trouserlegs at the ankle, but it did little good when we were caught on deck in water waist deep. Many times the whole watch would be caught at the leebraces when the ship would roll way down to leeward, taking tons of green water aboard and washing everybody off their feet. There would be a mad scramble to catch hold of something and hold on like grim death while the water swirled and tugged, as though determined to claim a victim. The scuppers were entirely inadequate to cope with the volume of water that kept pouring on deck, and work, other than working the sails, was out of the question. It was constant "stand by," and lucky was the watch which could take its four hours below without interruption.

We missed the bogie severely. It had been the only means we had to dry our clothes. We would come off watch soaked through, take off our boots and oilskins, then our clothes and underwear, wring them out and put them on again. Then we climbed into our bunks wrapped in our blankets and hoped that body-heat would do the rest. The gale might howl and shriek outside, punctuated by the thunder of water crashing on deck, but we dropped off to sleep immediately, only to be roused four hours later and repeat the cycle. Our clothes would be still damp, but on with the boots and oilskins and on deck, slashing one's way to the wheel along the life lines, to be greeted by the same gray rollers under leaden skies rearing themselves threateningly to windward as if intent on overwhelming this foolhardy intruder. A two-hour turn at the wheel fully exposed to the icy wind, which seemed to explore every cranny and fold in our clothes, then became torture.

"Peggy's" task of getting the grub from the galley was

at this time a daily adventure, and several times we saw our dinner washed down the deck with "Peggy" having a desperate hold somewhere to keep from following it. The steward's task was even more perilous. To bring the chow from the galley to the cabin he had to traverse the whole length of the deck. Our dislike of the steward grew daily, and the sight of him, clutching the lifeline under his arm while holding onto a dishpan in one hand and a coffee pot in the other, trying to keep his footing, always filled us with unholy glee.

There were days of respite, when the wind moderated and slanted enough to the south or north so that the ship could inch her way to the west. The seas ran in enormous swells even in moderate weather. With the prevailing westerly wind the seas never had much chance to calm down.

One morning a weary port-watch went below at eight bells (four A.M.). The previous afternoon the wind had freshened considerably and sails had been shortened. By nightfall it was blowing a full gale again with alternating gusts of sleet and rain. By midnight the wind was of hurricane strength. We got out of our oilskins and boots and dropped into our bunks fully dressed. I was damp and uncomfortable, and tossed restlessly in my bunk when there came a report like the cracking of a gun. It roused every one and we were already getting into our oilskins again when a fellow from the deckwatch stumbled into the focs'le.

"All hands on deck. The lower foretopsail has given way." From aloft came a staccato noise like machinegun fire and we could feel the tremor of the foremast. The mate in glistening oilskins came to the focs'le door.

"All hands aloft and furl the topsail!"

It was pitch dark as we tumbled out of the focs'le door onto a slippery deck, and clawed our way to the weather foreshrouds. The gale moaned and howled through the rigging and with the slatting and banging of the damaged sail, it was pandemonium. The deckwatch was already aloft, along with the apprentices, the second mate, and the bosun and the carpenter. Slowly, painfully we made our way up the weather rigging, over the futtock shrouds and joined the others on the sleet-covered yard. On the way up the wind tore the southwester off my head.

There we were, twenty men strung out along the slippery topsail yard, clinging desperately to the jackstay and trying to cope with a demon in the form of a sail. It had blown clean out of its bottom leach and was standing out horizontally from the yard, snapping with whiplash cracks. It was frozen stiff and impossible to get hold of. The ship rolled terribly, the foreyard arm to leeward almost touching the crest of the huge waves thundering away to leeward. As though to tease us, there would be an occasional lull and we would get hold of a fold in the canvas, only to have the gale, with renewed fury, tear the canvas from our grasp and leave us with bloody fingernails. It was all we could do to keep our footing on the sleet-covered footrope and limited our effort to merely holding on to the jackstay. We had lost all track of time when the mate appeared by the futtock shrouds, yelling to us to cut the sail free from the jackstay. Never was an order more welcome. It took only a few slashes with sheath knives and the gale did the rest. With a final demoniacal roar the sail tore itself loose and disappeared in the spume and welter to leeward.

DINNER FOR THE AFTERGUARD or THE CAPTAIN'S DINNER

It had been a nightmare.

Descending from the yard I found my southwester. It had been blown against the junction of a shroud and ratline and the pressure of the wind had kept it there. We had been on the yard almost two hours!

To save a few widths of canvas, the captain had been willing to keep his entire crew on the yard under almost impossible conditions, where he might easily have lost a man or two overboard, pitched from their slippery perch. We were a sore outfit when we got back into the focs'le and heaped curses and maledictions upon the ship and the captain. When "Peggy" came back from the galley with a steaming pot of coffee, and we sat down to our breakfast of maggoty hardtack and coffee, it added to our resentment. My watch, the port-watch, felt itself especially abused. We had been on deck from midnight to four in the morning, were roused out at around six to fight the sail, and now had to take the deck-watch again from eight A.M. to eight bells, noon.

As the day wore on there was no moderation in the gale; if anything it increased and it seemed as if the *Gwydyr Castle* was as much under as above the water. We hung oilbags in the rigging to smooth the waters around the ship and to prevent, if possible, breaking waves from crashing onto the ship's deck. They were bags made of sail canvas, containing about two quarts of oil, and were punctured in the bottom with a sail needle to let the oil seep out slowly. Hung in both fore and main rigging, they smoothed the waters somewhat, but the ship rolled so badly that the deck was never free of the green water she scooped up to leeward and to windward.

We were standing by under the shelter of the focs'le-head, a disgruntled lot, glumly watching the tumultu-ous waters around us, when we saw the mate, clawing his way forward along the life lines. He came up to us.

"The fore royal is working loose from its gaskets. One of you go up and fix it."

None of us were anxious to go, but as I happened to be nearest the mate when he gave his order I went over to weatherside and began to climb up to the gallant mast and royal yard. The force of the gale kept me pressed against the rigging, giving a feeling of comparative security, but when I stepped on to the footrope of the royal yard the wind kept tearing and tugging at me and I was forced to take a grim hold until I could get my breath. The rolling of the ship was bad enough on deck, but up here, almost a hundred feet above the deck, the motion was accentuated tenfold. I was tossed on a wide arc from one side to the other, and had to hold desperately to keep from being pitched off into space. I made the sail snug, tightened each gasket as well as I could under the conditions and then got off the yard, stopping on the gallant crosstrees to stop the pounding of my heart. I had a bird's-eye view of the whole scene and it was a beautiful sight, awe-inspiring in its grandeur. The skies had cleared somewhat and there were patches of blue amongst the driven clouds. The ship seemed to be wallowing in a sea of greenish milk; ranks of huge waves bore down on the ship from windward, breaking with a thunderous roar. Spume and spindrift blotted out the horizon, merging sea and sky in a gray vapor. An albatross appeared hovering around the ship and gliding quite close. He was motionless except for his head and eyes, and almost insulting in his indifference to the howling gale. The whole scene was so breathtaking that for the time being I was unaware of all the dangers and the hardships, lost in the overpowering display of the elements unchained.

At eight bells noon, we were relieved by the starboard-watch and after chow we climbed into our bunks to sleep the sleep of the exhausted. Towards evening the gale seemed to moderate, but it increased during the night, and the next morning the storm was again at its height. The ship was hove to under her main lower topsail and a small triangular sail rigged on the mizzen. We watched the topsail anxiously, hoping it wouldn't give under the strain as had the foretopsail. Going aft to relieve the man at the wheel, or lookout, was a hazardous trip even in daytime, but on a pitch-dark night, groping one's way aft along the lifelines and sensing suddenly the rearing of a mountainous sea to windward was enough to create panic in the stoutest heart.

The sailors' tempers were getting short. The constant discomfort in wet clothes, bad food, raw cold combined to make them curse the ship, the captain, the steward and themselves for being such fools as to ship on a sailing ship. Any one who did that when there were jobs ashore was crazy, and it was the last time they would ever ship out again. Resolutions always made under extreme circumstances and almost always forgotten when the emergency was past and life aboard became normal again.

It was while the crew was in such a semi-mutinous mood that the second mate appeared one afternoon where the deck-watch was huddled by the focs'lehead. Nobody said anything, ignoring his presence since he obviously had no order to give. Then he broke the silence.

"Well, boys, this is terrible. I don't ever remember a blow like this. We'll be lucky if we live through it." If he looked for sympathy, he had come to the wrong place.

The men felt too sore against the afterguard. Williams, the Welshman, suddenly burst out:

"Ah, get the hell aft where you belong. Don't come around here with your bellyaching."

The second mate looked rather surprised, but sensing our sullen, indifferent mood, he had no comeback, and left our group to wend his way aft again.

Like all bad things, this gale too came to an end. We bent on a new lower foretopsail and before very long were making some progress towards the west under a favorable slant of wind. We had hoisted both upper topsails and set the foresail and spanker, and when the mate came with orders to loosen and set the topgallantsails, our morale picked up considerably. Nothing like a fair slant of wind and seeing the ship actually making headway on its proper course to counteract the numbing sense of futility born while battling a headwind and gale at the same time. Our respite lasted about twenty-four hours. Then when the skipper ordered the topgallantsails furled, we knew he was getting ready for another blow. Sure enough before nightfall the ship was again under storm sail. Was there never to be an end to this misery and the everlasting gales?

By the time a dismal dawn outlined the horizon, the captain's precautions had been justified, and the ship was in the grip of a full gale. It blew without let-up all day and all night. The next dawn saw no abatement, but the skies were clearing and the sun broke through an occasional rift in the clouds. The captain made observations and decided to put the ship on the other tack. Both watches were called to stand by the braces. The wheel was put down to bring the ship up into the wind, but she came so far and no farther. There she hung stubbornly. She simply wouldn't tack.

After seeing the futility of that maneuver, all hands were called aft on the poop. Since the ship wouldn't tack, the captain was going to wear ship, *i.e.*, let her fall off before the wind and bring her up on the other tack. The wheel was put up and the ship fell off rapidly before the wind. It was a risky maneuver with a stiff, sluggish ship like the *Gwydyr Castle*, especially with an enormous sea running. She would be for a minute or so in the trough of the sea, a dangerous position at any time, and would she still be as stubborn in coming up on the other tack? There were some agonizing moments when we thought that we and the ship were doomed, and that along with hundreds of other ships the *Gwydyr Castle* would find Cape Horn her graveyard. While wallowing in the trough of the sea a huge comber crashed amidships, filling the deck from stem to stern, only the masts sticking out of a welter of white water, and the focs'lehead and the top of the deck-house looking like small waveswept islands. But the ship gradually righted herself, and slowly came up on the other tack. The crisis was passed.

We went down onto the main deck to tighten all the lee braces, and it was during this operation that the old sailmaker almost lost his life. He was really too old to be on deck under such conditions of weather and sea, but he was a proud old fellow, and thought himself, in spite of his years, as good a sailor as any of us, if not a better one. He had gone on the poop with us to lend a hand with whatever maneuver was required and when he went down to the main deck, along with the crew to attend to the braces, he made his way forward along the weatherside, knowing that a ship hove to will always take more water aboard to leeward than to windward. But his calculations were wrong, for a sea broke over the windward bulwark and broke his grip on the life line, washing him off his feet down to leeward. We had all scampered to safety on top of the fiferail circling the mainmast. There was no sight of the old sailmaker and the cry went up, "Man overboard!" We scanned the waters to leeward, but there was no sign of him. Then the ship rolled back to windward, shifting the water, and there, wedged in between the bulwarks and a reserve spar lashed alongside of them, was the sailmaker. We made a human chain and extricated him with some difficulty, as the water, shifting back and forth with each roll, alternately hid and revealed him. He was unconscious when we took him to his cabin, but we were able to revive him and warned him to keep to his cabin and off the deck. If he had been washed overboard, that would have been the end, as in such a sea it was impossible to launch a boat.

We all went back to the focs'le. "Peggy" had wheedled a pot of hot coffee out of the cook, and we were sitting around, when a fellow put his head in the focs'le with the electrifying cry, "A ship!" We all rushed on deck, some onto the focs'lehead and others into the rigging. We hadn't seen another ship for months, and it was a welcome sight. But how we envied the men on her! It was blowing a gale and we were fighting into the teeth of it. The other ship was under short sails also but she was driving before the wind, homeward bound. That westerly gale was poison to us, but manna from heaven to her. She was soon out of sight, and we were more than ever conscious of what still lay before us.

And so the days and weeks dragged by in their deadly monotony of ice, sleet, snow squalls, bitter cold and biting winds, wet clothes, shivering turns at the wheel and the lookout, and fighting stiff-frozen canvas on slippery footropes; death always there, close to one's elbow, waiting only for a single moment of carelessness to claim its victim.

There were, of course, lulls in the stormy weather, when we took the little chances for diversion which offered themselves. Beyond standing by, working the sails, furling them before a gale and setting them again after it had blown itself out, the spell at the wheel and the lookout, there was no other work to be done. We would stand by under the focs'lehead and relieve our boredom by plaiting sennit from rope yarn. Occasionally we found amusement and diversion in trying to catch Cape pigeons and albatross. The Cape pigeon is a friendly and gregarious sea bird, much smaller than a sea gull. They appeared quite frequently in flocks and swarmed around the ship, always alert to anything that might be thrown overboard. They received scant pickings from the *Gwydyr Castle*. The sailmaker, wise to all tricks, showed us how to catch them. We got a small piece of pork rind with a little fat attached and tied it to a length of sail twine. When we threw it overboard the pigeons would swoop down en masse, filling the air with their rather musical cries, and fighting and squabbling over the tidbit. When there was a cloud of fluttering wings hovering over the bait, the sailor holding the line would suddenly haul taut and pull the line aboard. More often than not a bird or two would have their wings entangled in the line and find themselves prisoners. We tested the first birds we caught for their edibility, but found them as rancid and fishy to the taste as boobies, so limited ourselves after that to the sport of catching and releasing them. They didn't seem to mind the experience or perhaps their greed conquered their fear, for they always came back.

Catching the albatross was a different matter and required careful preparations. Albatross appeared alone, or at the most in pairs. They hovered in the vicinity of the ship, but never as close as the Cape pigeons, which seemed utterly without fear. Again it was the old sailmaker who showed us how to fool the albatross. We procured a tin can from the cook, removed the top and bottom, and cut it vertically. It was pounded flat and cut into a triangular shape, about twice the length of the width of its base. Then an inner triangular section was cut out, care being taken that the inside angle of the point of the triangle should be very acute and sharp. Then both sides of the triangle were covered with strips of salt pork rind, fastened with wire. A foot of wire was fastened to a hole punctured in the base of the triangle and a stout line attached to it. As the fishing must be done astern, we had to get permission from the captain to fish from the poop. The watch would go aft to watch the fun. The triangular bait was tossed overboard and the line paid out until the bait floated about fifty yards astern. Soon the albatross would appear, hovering high in the air above the bait, then come swooping down, lighting in the water close to the bait, which was alluring enough to allay his suspicions and tempt him to worry it. Then it was up to the fisherman at the end of the line. When he thought that the bird had a firm hold of the morsel, he and the fellows with him would suddenly pull the line taut and haul it hand over hand. The object was to catch the albatross's beak in the sharp inside corner of the triangular bait and to jam it fast. The beak of an albatross is curved at the end like an eagle's, and has some flexibility.

It was not an easy trick to accomplish and most of the birds worked themselves free. To keep a constant and equal tension on the line was almost impossible when the water was at all rough, and the bird took advantage of the slightest slack. As soon as the albatross felt himself propelled through the water against his will, he would struggle furiously, braking with both his webbed feet and his enormous wings, trying to get rid of the thing which kept his head imprisoned. The most ticklish part of the operation came when the bird was finally brought up to the overhang of the quarter-deck. Then it had to be lifted out of the water and quickly hauled up. It was during this last stage most birds freed themselves, but we landed quite a few successfully. As soon as the albatross was on deck he was a helpless prisoner. Even freed from the bait he was unable to escape. His enormous wingspread made it impossible for him to launch himself from a flat surface. Very shortly he became seasick and disgorged everything he had devoured during the previous hours.

There is a widespread belief that sailors are superstitious about the bad luck that followed the killing of an albatross. Perhaps Coleridge's "Ancient Mariner" had something to do with that belief, but with the possible exception of Birmingham, the British sailor, none of us had ever heard of Coleridge or the "Ancient Mariner." We never considered the albatross for food, having tried other sea birds and found them unpalatable, but the sailmaker told us how sailors had utilized the big webbed feet of the albatross for tobacco pouches, his long, hollow wing bones for pipe stems and the long, curved beak for walking-stick handles. The first albatross we caught was killed for such utilitarian purposes, but most of us felt rather badly about it, and all the birds subsequently caught were released.

We were not a superstitious outfit anyway. On many ships Finns were considered a hoodoo, and prolonged spells of headwind were blamed on the presence of Finns in the focs'le, but I never heard such a thing mentioned aboard the *Gwydyr Castle*. We had three Finns in the focs'le. They were the best sailors of the entire outfit, and one of them, Fatty Ecklund, I liked best of the entire crew.

It had been almost two months since we had left the Falklands behind. Two months of purgatory in a watery hell, and as far as we in the focs'le knew, it might go on forever, when one morning the deck-watch came bursting in the focs'le and roused us with the magic cry of "Land! Land!" We all piled out on deck and there to starboard was Cape Horn. The skies had cleared during the night and the *Gwydyr Castle* was sailing past the cape, full and bye, under a blue sky. A marvelous sight to us. The wind was fair and fresh and the ship herself acted as though she had awakened from a bad dream, dipping and lifting into the blue Pacific swell. The mainsail was unfurled and sheeted home for the first time in two months, and by nightfall the ship was plowing along at a good clip under full sails. As if to make amends for its wicked behavior off Cape Horn, the wind stayed fresh and fair as we sailed up along the west coast of South America.

Day by day we approached warmer latitudes, and we took our clothes and mattresses on deck to air and dry out. What a comfort to feel once again a dry shirt on one's back! Under cloudless skies we drove north and a general feeling of optimism replaced the sullen resentment we had harbored against everything and everybody connected with the ship. Even an epidemic of carbuncles and salt-water boils didn't dampen our spirits much. The skies were too blue, the sun too warm. The fair wind held and the leaden seas and skies off Cape Horn became soon only an unpleasant memory. Even the equatorial regions were kind to us, and it wasn't until we reached the Bay of Panama that we were delayed by a week of calm. But that too came to an end, and one afternoon after a voyage of over five months from Cardiff, the *Gwydyr Castle* dropped anchor off Panama.

CHAPTER
4

PANAMA TO PUGET SOUND

PANAMA, TROPICAL Panama! What romantic visions I had conjured up about it, and how far short it fell of my expectation! We anchored quite a distance from Panama City, in the vicinity of an island. As soon as we dropped anchor, while we were still aloft furling the sails, there appeared a swarm of bumboats. The boatsmen were not permitted to board the ship and they waited alongside until everything aloft had been made shipshape. When we reached the deck a clamor went up from them, each boatman trying to drown out his rivals. They offered all sorts of tropical fruits, bananas, mangoes, lemons, limes, oranges, plus cigars, cigarettes and the usual line of obscene French postcards. Several of them also had parrots and monkeys for sale. The captain allowed us to draw against our wages to the extent of five shillings per man. We soon exhausted that limit.

The first thing I did was to drop a fishing line overboard, and the result was rather disastrous. I got a good bite and hauled in the line in great excitement. The fish flopped on deck and I grabbed it firmly to dislodge the hook, only to receive the spiny dagger of the fish squarely in the palm of my left hand. I had never seen nor heard of a catfish before, and was totally ignorant of its means of self-defense. The wound was very painful and it incapacitated me for several days, much to the disgust of the mate, who needed every hand to begin the unloading of our coal cargo.

We had hoped that the skipper would avail himself of the cheap labor ashore to help us discharge the cargo, and were a disgruntled lot when we found out we were to do it all ourselves. The donkey engine, carried abaft the mainmast, was made ready by the carpenter, but it broke down the first day, and no one seemed able to put it into working order again. Luck certainly was against us. Every pound of coal had to be discharged by hand. One half of the crew worked in the hold, filling the baskets with coal, and the other half on deck by the hand winches, hoisting the full baskets up and emptying them into the lighters alongside. We worked from six in the morning until six in the evening in a stifling, oppressive heat. The men at the winches were protected from the blistering sun by tarpaulins rigged over their heads. The work was rotated so that one gang shoveled coal in the hold one day, and was at the winches the next. No one could grouse that any one had an easier job than the other. We all stripped to the waist, and consumed enormous quantities of oatmeal water, but it was stifling work in the hold and backbreaking work at the winches. We would emerge out of the hold at the end of the day looking like shiny, black Ethiopians. Coal dust got into everything and personal cleanliness became a thing of the past. At first, as soon as work was finished, we stripped and jumped overboard for a refreshing and cleansing swim, but after a couple of big sharks were seen in the vicinity of the ship, only the few foolhardy amongst us took the risk, and they didn't venture very far from the Jacob's ladder slung over the side. The rest of us lined up along the bulwarks and doused each other with buckets of water hauled from the side. The steward provided fresh meat and yams, which, though monotonous as a diet, were a welcome change from the eternal salt beef and pork.

The Panama of today is as different from the Panama of 1902 as white is from black. Then it was a pest hole. Yellow fever, malaria and smallpox were rampant. It wasn't very long before men were laid low by malaria. The outbreak infuriated the captain, who would come into the focs'le where the sick men lay in their bunks, and openly accuse them of malingering. He got even with them by dosing them liberally with Black Draught, that old stand-by of sulphur and molasses. We received no shore leave except for the ones who became so ill they had to be taken ashore to receive medical attention.

One Sunday we went aft for permission to take the dinghy and row over to the island near which the *Gwydyr Castle* was anchored. To our surprise, permission was granted, and we spent most of the day tramping over its steep paths, which wound their way through jungle growth, and led here and there to small clearings with a few thatched huts. In one clearing we came across what must have been a clan or family gathering. Strung between two palmettos hung a hammock, and in it reposed a huge colored woman dressed in nondescript garments of gaudy colors. Grouped around her were about fifteen or twenty people of all shades of brown and black, and of all ages and sizes. Weaving in and out amongst the group were naked children, scrawny chickens, a few gaunt, mangy-looking dogs and some razor-backed hogs. Our surprise on coming upon them was fully equaled by theirs at seeing a group of white men suddenly emerge from the jungle. We spoke no Spanish, and they no English, but we tried to point out to them that we were from the ship anchored near by, and departed.

Looking at the same jungle growth soon palled on us. As there seemed to be little else on the island and the heat began to oppress us, we went back to the dinghy which we loaded with bananas we had gathered, and returned to the ship. Even so it was a break in the numbing monotony of our existence, but our hopes of repeating the excursion were dashed next day when word came from aft that the authorities had put the island under quarantine, as smallpox had broken out amongst its inhabitants.

During our stay in Panama no other sailing ship arrived, and the few small steamers that visited the harbor were all of the coastal variety. All in all Panama was a great disillusionment to every one and we all looked forward to the day when our cargo would be discharged and we could leave that miasmic place behind. Our only real diversion was to get ashore, and that was denied us. There was no reading matter. Some of the men had musical instruments aboard and they helped to while away the evenings, but by eight o'clock, we usually were all in our bunks.

The voyage from Cardiff to Panama, due to our difficult and prolonged stay off Cape Horn, had taken much longer than either the captain or the steward had expected, and the latter went ashore to investigate the possibility of replenishing our food supply. The city of Panama was not the most propitious place to find the sort of supplies we needed. There was little deep-water shipping, and it would have been hardly worth while for a shipchandler to set up shop. After scouring around the city, the steward had a windfall. He got news of some British Admiralty stores, stored in a warehouse, and he bought a large supply of them. When they were brought alongside, and we unloaded them under the supervision of the steward, Liverpool Jack was skeptical about their quality, and openly accused the steward of having bought Admiralty stores which had been declared unfit for use in the British Navy. How else could he have gotten hold of them? The steward indignantly denied it, and we had no way of knowing, but when the flour and salt meat eventually came to the galley, and from there to the focs'le, we were all convinced that Liverpool Jack's suspicions had been well founded. There was no doubt then that the steward had done an exceedingly good stroke of business for the ship's owner, at the crew's expense.

The wearisome toil of discharging our coal was coming to an end, and before the last of it had been unloaded, lighters with ballast came alongside. There was no cargo to be taken on in Panama, and we had to sail in ballast, to whatever port the captain received orders to go. The ballast consisted of broken stone and rubble, the stones, all sizes, from big boulders down, and was not the best kind of ballast to have in the hold, should the ship run into really tough weather. We leveled it out amidships in the hold, and secured it with planking, which was held down with props wedged in under the steel deck beams.

The cargo was finally discharged, but no word had been received as to our next destination. Every evening we awaited the return of the captain's gig, hoping for news of our departure, only to be disappointed. Meanwhile we started in to clean the ship, scrubbing the deck and paintwork from bow to stern and even washing the masts down. The sails were unbent and lowered on deck and replaced by light weather canvas. Finally came the happy afternoon when the captain's gig returned from shore with the welcome news that he had received instuctions. We were to sail up the Pacific coast for Esquimault, British Columbia, and there await orders. The next morning we manned the capstan on the focs'lehead with a will, getting up the anchor, and with a light breeze hardly filling our sails, we turned our back on Panama and sailed out into Panama Bay.

America! It was a magic word to me, the land of plenty, the land of opportunity, fabulous in every way. While in the Seminary some years before, I had asked my benefactress for a book about America for Christmas, and my wish had been granted. It was a two-volume affair, profusely illustrated with hundreds of photographs, and became my prize possession. Now before long, I was actually to step on her shores. We all looked forward to it, and several of the crew, including Liverpool Jack, were quite frank in saying that they would leave the ship at the first opportunity. Some of them would have jumped ship in Panama, but for the lack of a chance to do so, and the fact that it was hardly a good place for a sailor to be on the beach.

Light winds helped us out of Panama Bay, but soon they failed us, and day after day we drifted along on a glassy sea, only occasionally ruffled by a faint catspaw promising a breeze that didn't come. We drifted for over a month between five and ten degrees north, and spent our first Christmas under a broiling sun, the deck so hot that the marine glue in the deck seams boiled up in big blobs. The ocean was dead calm and the horizon lost in the mingled glare of the sea's surface and the heat haze. It was an intensified repetition of our experience in the doldrums of the Atlantic. The trimming of the yards, the clewing up and then sheeting home of the sails, all the maneuvers of trying to catch a breeze that never materialized, seemed purposeless. It got on every one's nerves, and tempers became frayed. The climax came when some of the provisions the steward had purchased in Panama reached the focs'le. The salt beef and pork were both rancid, and smelled to high heaven, and the flour for our biweekly soft bread was mouldy.

It was on Christmas Day our tempers burst. We had lost our prospective Christmas dinner when Dennis was washed overboard off the Horn, but to celebrate the day the cook had baked bread with prunes in it, no doubt as a sort of substitute for plumduff. When "Peggy" cut into the soggy concoction, and we found it almost unpalatable, Liverpool Jack took the dishpan and went to the galley, followed by most of the crew. When the cook came to the galley door and stuck his head out, we told him just what we thought of him. The cook was hot-tempered himself, and answered back in kind, and insults were pandied back and forth. One of the sailors yanked the dishpan out of Jack's hands and threw it into the cook's face, whereupon the latter grabbed up a big carving knife, and brandishing it stepped out on deck. Then the riot started. One of the men got a belaying pin and hit him on the arm, making him drop the knife. The cook retreated aft, the men following, threatening and abusing him. The mate was attracted by the noise and ordered the men to go forward, but they were in a mutinous mood and began to abuse him too. It wasn't until the captain himself appeared on the scene that the men returned forward, though not without cursing the ship and everybody aft, especially the steward, to a fare-thee-well.

The steward had kept out of sight during the disturbance, and wisely so. The cook, thoroughly scared, went back to the galley and an uneasy peace reigned once more on the ship. When "Peggy" next came to the galley, the cook told him that he couldn't help the food. He did his best with what the steward provided, but it was all bad. We made our peace with the cook, but towards the steward we had only an abiding hatred.

One morning we found another ship on the horizon, a big four-masted barque, and we were in sight of each other for three days, though never near enough to identify her. We seemed like two phantom ships, drifting sometimes almost out of sight of each other, and then again fairly close. One morning she had disappeared, and we felt more deserted between sea and sky than ever.

We fished every chance we got and caught enough to eke out our scanty and questionable fare. The captain even allowed us to go out in the dinghy after some of the huge turtles, seemingly asleep on the surface of the water, but we never had the luck to catch one.

One day we had a windfall. A breeze had sprung up, and once again we heard the swishing of the bow through the water, and the humming of straining sheets. A school of porpoises appeared off our starboard, and when close to the ship cavorted under our bow, jumping and gamboling playfully. One of the apprentices named "Ginger," because of his carroty hair, went aft to the mate, and returned with a harpoon. We rigged a manila rope to its shaft and passed the harpoon to Ginger, who had secured himself under the bowsprit, free of all running and standing gear.

The lad was no harpooner, and a porpoise is a small and elusive target compared with a whale, but miracles happen, and quite unexpectedly the harpoon sank in the back of one of the porpoises. There was great excitement. Some of us were gathered by the starboard fore-shrouds where the manila rope had one turn taken around a belaying pin. When the porpoise was struck, it immediately sheered away to starboard at quite a clip, taking up the slack in the rope. We slowly paid out the rope around the belaying pin, and when the harpoon seemed to hold, we began to haul in. We brought the struggling porpoise alongside, and, with the aid of a block fastened in the forerigging, hoisted it out of the water and on deck. It was hardly over the rail when the harpoon tore loose. It had been only by extraordinary luck that we had landed him at all. We hung it by the tail in the forerigging right away, and the cook butchered it. The porpoise is a mammal, and warmblooded, and when the cook was through eviscerating it the carcass looked not unlike that of a pig. For once we had a generous supply of fresh meat. It tasted like young beef, and much better than any of the fresh meat dished out to us

in Panama. We preserved the entire skin, which is very tough and makes almost unbreakable shoelaces, and lacings of all kinds. We tried again and again to catch another, but had no more success.

We availed ourselves of any opportunity for diversion from the daily monotony. One night I had my turn at the wheel from four bells to eight bells midnight. About half an hour before being relieved I saw a big black bird light on the main truck. It evidently intended to roost there for the night, and I decided to catch it if I could. At eight bells I was relieved, and immediately went to the mainrigging and up the mast. Standing on the royal yard I could see the bird just above me. I shinnied up along the royal halyard and finally reached the truck. There I stood, my bare feet clutching the small projection around which the royal backstay was fastened, and with one arm around the truck. Then commenced a fencing match between the bird and me. The bird had become aware of my presence and made lunges at me with its wicked-looking beak, while I tried to grasp it around the neck. Just as I was on the point of abandoning the enterprise, I succeeded, and pulled the bird off its perch. It struggled furiously with both feet and wings, but I managed to keep my hold until I had descended back onto the yard. There I tightened my belt, drew my stomach in and brought the head of the bird inside my belt and let my stomach out again. I then shinnied down the royal backstay, the bird's big wings beating the air. Once on deck again, I took the bird forward and put it in the pig pen, to have its ultimate fate decided the next day.

It was a big frigate bird, with its wings out of all proportion to the size of its body. We decided to keep it, on the chance that we might capture some boobies that evening. We got a couple that were roosting on the main topsail yard, and put them in the other pig pen. During the dog-watch of the next day we released the birds on deck, hoping for the equivalent of a cock fight, but while the frigate bird will attack a booby in mid-air, and relieve it of its catch, it didn't seem disposed to stage a fight for our amusement, and we released them all.

Breezes were more frequent now and, although very light, they gave promise of steadier winds to come. We had reached ten degrees north, and coming on deck one morning watch, we found the ship heeling slightly to leeward, rising and dipping with a bone in her teeth. This looked like more than a promise, and when orders came to replace the light with the heavy canvas, we turned to with a will. At last there was to be an end of the stagnant drifting. The wind was fair and increased in strength, and the doldrums off the Bay of Panama were a thing of the past. Then came several weeks of steady winds and fair sailing up along the California coast.

After crossing forty degrees north there was a change in the weather. Gray, scudding clouds replaced sunny skies. The wind increased and royals and topgallantsails were taken in, and at the end of another twenty-four hours the *Gwydyr Castle* was reduced to foresail, the two lower topsails, fore and mizzen staysails and a reefed spanker. The wind increased to gale strength, and the ship labored hard in the steadily mounting sea. Being in ballast, and high out of the water, not much water was shipped, but the fury of the gale increased, and in the dog-watch both watches were sent aloft to take in the foresail. By nightfall the *Gwydyr Castle* was bucking the gale under only her two topsails and the forestaysail.

During the prolonged doldrums, the old sailmaker had been busy making a brand-new lower topsail to replace the one which had been blown to tatters off Cape Horn. It was a beautiful job, and old "Sails" was justly proud of it, little realizing that it would act as a canopy when we consigned his body to a watery grave.

My watch had gone below at eight bells (four A.M.). It seemed to me that I had barely fallen asleep when I was shaken awake by the little Finn. He stood on the settee running along the lower bunks, dressed in his glistening oilskins and was bending over me, with a look of fear in his eyes. He had just been relieved at the wheel, and in going forward had stumbled over the body of a man lying across the deck just abaft the galley. It frightened him, and he ran into the focs'le. My bunk being nearest the door, he roused me up. I quickly awakened the other fellows, and we went out on deck, preceded by the little Finn.

By this time word had spread around the ship of what had happened, and both watches gathered around the body. There, by the dim light of a lantern, lay the old sailmaker clad only in his woolen underwear, sprawled out, his arms extended and his toes still resting on the coaming of his cabin door. He was lying face down, close to a big ringbolt fastened in the deck, his head in a dark pool of blood winding its way in rivulets towards the lee scuppers. The gale was blowing a dirge through the rigging, spindrift drove across the deck-house from the weather side and the sea roared and crashed around the ship. A fitting setting for the death of an old sailor.

The mate appeared on the scene, followed by the captain, and they examined the body for possible signs of life. There was no pulse and no sign of respiration when the mate held a small pocket mirror to old

THE DEATH WATCH

"Sails' " mouth. The captain pronounced him dead and ordered us to pick up the body and lay it out temporarily in the sail-locker in the after part of the forward deckhouse. A couple of short planks were gotten out of the hold and we made a rudimentary bier amongst the spare sails. When the body had been deposited on the planks, Liverpool Jack spoke up. He thought some one ought to stay in there with "Sails" if by any chance he should show signs of life. The mate replied that in his opinion the man was dead as dead could be, but it was all right with him if some one wanted to keep a death watch, and thought that Liverpool Jack might stand the first watch. Nobody seemed very anxious to be cooped up in the cramped quarters with a corpse, but a Swede finally agreed reluctantly to stand the first watch. The lantern was passed in to him and it was an eerie sight, with the yellow glow of the lantern playing on the rough-hewn features of the old sailmaker, and accentuating the big, bloody hole in his forehead just above the right eye. Rigor mortis had not yet set in, and we crossed his big gnarled hands, one over the other, on his chest.

We went back to the focs'le in the dim light of early dawn and retired to our bunks with uneasy minds. There seemed to be a hoodoo over the ship. First we lost Tim Sullivan off the royal yard, then we had that terrible time off Cape Horn, and now the old sailmaker's death in what seemed to us a rather mysterious manner.

I found it impossible to go back to sleep, and when shortly, at eight bells (eight A.M.), the deck-watch came into the focs'le for their coffee and hardtack, discussion became general. It was a situation made to order for that natural sea lawyer, Liverpool Jack, and it wasn't long before the discussion became acrimonious. He advanced the opinion that there might have been foul play. The cook and the sailmaker were always quarreling, and he, Jack, wouldn't put it beyond the cook to have bashed in the old fellow's head. Jack was a born trouble maker, and anything he could do to embarrass the afterguard was all right with most of us. The scurvy treatment we got in respect to food wasn't conducive to loyalty. However, since Jack had joined the crew in Cardiff, there had been at best only a state of armed truce between him and me, and I now ridiculed his suggestion of foul play, and elaborated on my theory of how the accident happened, which seemed much more logical to me.

During the night the sailmaker had probably gotten out of his bunk to relieve himself. When he opened his cabin door, the deck was wet, and, clad as he was in only underwear and socks (the usual bunk attire), he didn't want to get wet, so stood inside the coaming to attend to it. It was blowing a gale and the ship was lurching and rolling violently. While he stood there, half asleep, supporting himself against the door-frame, the ship must have taken a sudden deep roll to leeward, and pitched him headlong out onto the deck, where he struck his head against the ringbolt. The fact that his toes were still inside the coaming when he was found, was, to me at least, conclusive proof that that was how it had happened. Most of the fellows agreed with my theory. Anyway it was certainly more comfortable to think that the old fellow died accidentally rather than through foul play, but the whole discussion only added to the antagonism between Jack and me, which some day I felt would come to a showdown. It was almost inevitable.

During my next watch on deck I took a turn at the

death watch. Now that it was light, none of us minded it very much. The sailmaker and I had been good friends. He had always been ready to teach me the things an able-bodied seaman had had to know in the days of his youth, when the rigging was all of rope, and the use of wire almost unknown. He had sailed the seas for over fifty years, and knew everything there was to be known about a ship and its rigging.

Word came from aft that the sailmaker would be buried at eight bells (four P.M.) that afternoon. We rigged a bier of planks, one end resting on the starboard rail amidships, and the other on a platform of barrels and boxes. The body of old "Sails" was carried out onto the main hatch, where, with half a dozen links of anchor chain at the feet, it was sewn into a shroud of sail canvas. At eight bells everybody assembled around the bier. The shrouded figure was covered with the British ensign, and the captain began to read the burial service. The only men not in the gathering were the man at the wheel and the cook. He watched the whole proceeding from the galley, leaning on his elbows on the closed lower half of the door, puffing away at his pipe.

It was a dramatic scene. The wind was blowing a gale and whipping spray across us from windward. Water was slashing around our feet, and up aloft, the lower maintopsail, the sailmaker's last job, was straining in its sheets. The captain finished reading the service, the flag was removed and the planks tilted up. As the body was committed overboard, the ship heeled hard over and green water rose up to meet it as if anxious to claim its own.

Back in the focs'le, Liverpool Jack was quick to point out that the cook hadn't attended the service. It had struck some of the sailors as rather queer to see the cook leaning on his elbows out of the galley door, a dirty cloth cap perched on his halo of hair, and a pipe in his mouth.

By the next morning the gale had moderated and the wind shifted fair, so we shook out the foresail and set the two upper topsails along with a jib and the spanker. We were all grouped around in the focs'le during the first dog-watch, when the second mate came to the focs'le door and said the skipper wanted one of us to come aft and add his signature to the account of the sailmaker's death and burial in the ship's log. Why he deemed such a procedure necessary, we didn't know, but Liverpool Jack immediately took it as more evidence that something was queer in the whole business. In no uncertain terms he said he wouldn't sign, and what he thought of any one who would. His tirade had its effect on the fellows, and none of them were willing to go aft. Then I began to ridicule Jack's assumptions again and the repartee became more sarcastic and abusive by the minute. It ended by my getting up and going to the captain's stateroom, where I put my signature as witness to the story of the sailmaker's death.

When I returned to the focs'le I was met with a mixed reception. Most of the sailors didn't care one way or another, but Jack had enough backing to greet me with jeering remarks, which grew more abusive, and he ended by calling me a "lickspittle." That was all that was needed to touch off the powder keg inside of me. I jumped across the table to where he was sitting below his bunk and began to throw punches at him. We were quickly separated, and both of us went out on deck, followed by the whole gang.

There were no preliminaries. We went for each other hammer and tongs. The ship was still pitching and rolling badly, and the deck was so slippery we found it hard to keep our feet. First one and then the other would miss a haymaker and the misspent force, aided by the roll of the ship, would land us in the scuppers. We stopped by mutual consent to take off our boots and renewed the battle in our stocking feet. We both hated each other, and it was a bitter fight. I became oblivious of his blows, and put all my accumulated resentment into every blow aimed at him. We both took severe punishment as the battle surged back and forth between the focs'lehead and the foremast.

Then came the break. I landed a heavy blow on Jack just at the moment when the ship took a deep roll to leeward. The force of the blow and the roll of the ship landed Jack hard against the fiferail around the foremast and he was "on the ropes." In my blind rage I rained blow after blow on him until the other fellows jumped in and put a stop to it. Jack was thoroughly beaten, though from appearances it would have been hard to pick the victor. Both my eyes began to swell, I was bleeding from the mouth, and both my hands were badly sprained. As usual after my spasms of rage, I became violently nauseated. There was no handshake afterwards, and we remained enemies until he jumped ship in Tacoma.

In a few days the weather turned fair again and we were on our course to Cape Flattery and Puget Sound. There was to be an auction of the sailmaker's effects, and one dog-watch we all went to the afterhatch where they were gathered in a pile. They were of firstrate quality, and the bidding became spirited. But we had no chance against Liverpool Jack, the Russian carpenter and two other sailors. They outbid everybody. It seemed logical on the part of the carpenter, who was about the same size as the sailmaker, but we couldn't see how Liverpool Jack and the two sailors could ever use any of "Sails'" clothes. We were pretty sure then that three of the crew meant to jump ship in our next port. They would have to leave their pay behind anyway, so didn't care how much was charged against their wages.

The whole affair was conducted in a rather hilarious atmosphere. I bid in the old fellow's dittybag, a beautifully made wooden box holding all his needles, thread, scissors, buttons, etc., everything needed to make and repair garments. I had it amongst my effects for years.

Like Tim Sullivan, the old sailmaker was soon forgotten. Deep-water sailors were always thrown together by accident. They might be full of mutual antipathy, but were forced to live together in the closest intimacy. Unless they were in different watches they couldn't get out of each other's sight and it was no wonder that tempers flared up quickly, and fist fights were a common occurrence. The sailmaker had been rather popular amongst us all, but he didn't belong to the focs'le gang, and, beyond its dramatic setting, his death left no lasting impression on most of us.

We were making steady progress along the west coast of Oregon when near disaster overtook the *Gwydyr Castle*. The barometer had taken a tumble and the captain had ordered the sails shortened until we were again reduced to lower topsails and a forestaysail. The wind increased by the minute, and when my watch came on deck, it was blowing a hurricane. High in the water, as we were, even the few sails carried were sufficient to keep the ship listing sharply to leeward. The seas rose to enormous size, making us all apprehensive. We were afraid of the ballast. It was stowed well enough, but would the shoring stand up under the hard laboring of the ship under the terrific stress of wind and sea?

After a hectic night our worst fears were realized early one morning when we, the watch below, were roused out of our sleep by a fearful rumbling and pounding down deep in the ship. The noise reached us like a galvanic shock and we tumbled out of our bunks and into our boots and oilskins even before a sailor of the deck-watch came bursting into the focs'le with the ominous cry, "All hands out and down the hold. The ballast is shifting!"

Nobody said a word, but we rushed on deck and aft, oblivious of the howling of the gale in the masts above us, conscious only of the ugly noises emanating from below. We had to claw our way aft on the sloping deck along the weather rail up to the small hatch below the break of the poop. The deck-watch had already gone below, followed by the apprentices, the carpenter, the bosun and the two mates. We descended one by one into the inferno below, the cook staying behind to close the hatch after us, and to stand guard by it. Only he, the captain and the man at the wheel remained above deck, while below every one else waged a life-and-death struggle in the dark hold, only faintly illuminated by two ship's lanterns.

The heavy rolling and pounding of the ship had loosened part of the shoring which held the planks covering the ballast. The rubble had begun to work loose and was starting to pile up to leeward. This had to be prevented at any cost. We worked frantically in the dim, yellow light of the lanterns to get control of the ballast where it had given way, and to re-enforce the planking where it still held the ballast within bounds, always on the alert for stray boulders which careened about with seemingly malignant intent. It was literally a matter of life or death. The ballast had to be gotten under control, or it meant the end of the ship. It also meant a personal and immediate end, if a boulder caught one of us off guard.

We worked on frantically, unaware of the passage of time, until we finally succeeded in averting the almost certain disaster. Not one of us escaped bruises and abrasions, and some had had narrow escapes with the flying boulders. Emerging on deck from that nightmare below, we almost welcomed the tempest around us.

Towards afternoon the gale moderated, and in the dog-watch we set the two upper topsails and shook loose and sheeted home the foresail. The next day the skies had cleared, though a big sea was still running and we headed towards Vancouver to find the entrance to Juan de Fuca Straits by Cape Flattery. Then the weather worsened again, and a blanket of fog descended over the waters. The fog lasted almost a week, preventing the captain from making observations. We beat back and forth in short tacks off Vancouver Island, always westerly, to avoid piling up on the rocky coast.

Fog is almost worse to a sailor than a gale. At least a gale is a known quantity and we know how to cope with it, but in fog you are blinded. The ship can be cut in two by a steamer, or if close to land, pile up on the rocks if the captain makes a miscalculation. When a sailor came forward after being relieved at the wheel and saying he was sure he heard the roaring of surf, we scoffed at him, and yet were somehow uneasy that it might be true. The fog had begun to wear on our nerves. It had been a long, dreary pull since we had left Panama, the long weeks of calm off the Bay of Panama, the death of the sailmaker, followed by the almost disastrous hurricane off Cape Flattery, and now, within sight of our goal, this fog.

Then relief came in the form of a Japanese steamer bound for Seattle. She loomed up out of the fog and we hailed her with signals whereupon she slowed down and came near enough to give the captain his position. The skipper had not been very far off in his dead reckoning. We were a little northwest of Cape Flattery, and corrected our position.

The fog dispersed gradually, and by next morning the skies were clear, and off to starboard was the welcome sight of land. The wind held steady and fair, taking us past the rocks at the entrance to Juan de Fuca Straits and up to the anchorage off Esquimault, British Columbia. Sails were shortened, the anchor dropped and the second leg of our voyage was a thing of the past.

CHAPTER

5

TACOMA TO CALLAO

NEXT MORNING the gig was lowered to take the captain and the steward ashore; the captain to notify the home office of our arrival and to get mail, and the steward to shop for fresh provisions, of which we were sorely in need. He returned in a few hours, and a welcome sight it was when "Peggy" brought a dishpan of fresh meat and potatoes from the galley for our noonday meal.

Towards evening a launch arrived alongside bringing back the captain. No orders had been received from the home office, and there were but few letters for the focs'le, but there was some news about the hurricane that almost sent the *Gwydyr Castle* to the bottom. Several ships were said to have piled up along the rocky coast, and a British man-of-war had been lost with all hands on board, some two hundred men.

There was a tremendous export of wheat and lumber out of Puget Sound, and we didn't expect to be anchored off Esquimault long. The captain returned to the ship one evening after we had been there about a week, with the news that we would leave in the morning for Tacoma to take on a cargo of wheat for Callao, Peru.

We had had no shore leave in Esquimault, much to our disgust. The captain undoubtedly suspected that some of the crew were just waiting for the opportunity to jump ship, and he took no chances in a port where it would be difficult to find replacements. In Tacoma it wouldn't matter, as that was a thriving port, crammed with sailing ships of all kinds and nationalities. The crew would not be required to attend to the loading of the cargo, and if any of the crew deserted, it would only benefit the owners, since practically a year's pay would be forfeited.

The next morning a tug came alongside, the anchor was hoisted, and we were off for Tacoma. The weather had cleared finally, and a blue sky and fresh breeze replaced the low hanging clouds, and fine drizzle, of the past few days. Puget Sound was a beautiful sight. At last I would set foot in the United States. Little did I dream then that within another year America would become my permanent home.

The tug took us up the Sound at a good clip, all of us were lining the bulwarks to watch the scene, and plan what we would do in Tacoma, when a motorboat appeared off our starboard bow, made a circle, and came alongside. It contained three men, one of them a hardboiled customer, dressed in what we called "shore clothes," and a derby tilted on one side of his head. He called for a rope, and we threw him the end of a brace, which he fastened to the bow of the launch. Then began his spiel.

"Where are you from?"

"Panama."

"How long have you been on this hooker?"

"About a year."

"What's she like? A limejuicer, ain't she?"

"Well, she's easy enough as far as work is concerned, but the food isn't fit for a dog, and they starve you besides."

"Hell! They always do. What you get a month?"

"Three pounds."

"Three pounds! That's fifteen dollars. You must be damned fools. That's about fifty cents a day. Hell! You can get three dollars a day anywhere around here working in the lumberyards. Why don't you get wise to yourselves and jump ship? We got a good boardinghouse. Good food and plenty of it. Steaks every day. I can get you a good job any time. No night watches, plenty of girls and plenty of fun. What about it? If any of you fellows want to quit right now, just get your bags and jump down into the boat. What do you say?"

None of us had any particular love for the ship and none at all for her owners or officers, but the colossal effrontery of that boardinghouse shark trying to get us to desert the ship while she was still underway, was too much even for those who intended to jump the ship in Tacoma. Besides there was one chance in a million the skipper might consent to pay them off. Liverpool Jack and a couple of others asked questions, and sensing that

his siren song had fallen at least on fertile ground, the boardinghouse runner promised to be at the dock when the *Gwydyr Castle* tied up to take on her cargo.

This was my first glimpse of what I learned later was a highly organized traffic in sailors. Fortunately that is all a thing of the past now. Sailors in coastwise shipping could easily be organized for their own protection, and there may have been such an organization on the Pacific Coast even then. Deep-water sailors were a different matter, however, and were preyed upon by all the sharks and harpies infesting the waterfronts of the world. The sailors were generally a tough, shiftless lot, drifters, here today, there tomorrow. They would spend a year or two in the deadly monotony of a ship's focs'le, constantly taking their chances with sudden death on both deck and yard, with bad food and low pay. Then they would find themselves ashore with one or two years' pay in their jeans and a few drinks were all that was needed to get them going, and their defenses down. Quite often, within a week or so, Jack would either be on the beach, or find himself in a strange focs'le on an outward-bound ship without the slightest idea how he got there. Sailors' boardinghouses with their crimps and runners, waterfront saloons with their knockout drops, ladies of easy virtue, expert at picking pockets! What chance did poor, dumb Jack have against that unholy crew?

Naturally all deep-water sailors were not like that. Swedish, Norwegian and German ships were usually manned by their own nationals, and had a different background. It was the British limejuicers that seemed to be manned by all the scum of the seven seas. On the *Gwydyr Castle*, only three men in the focs'le ever received any mail during the two years I was on her.

The traffic in sailors along Puget Sound was highly organized and cleverly managed. Roughly, this is how it worked. A ship would arrive at any of the Puget Sound ports, Tacoma, Seattle, Port Royal, Port Townsend, etc. The runners would come aboard, taking advantage of such dissatisfaction as existed aboard, and tempt the sailors to desert with alluring pictures of the delights of life ashore, good wages, good food, girls, drinking and dancing. The contrast between these conjurings and their miserable life aboard was so great that many sailors were tempted, and deserted their ships, leaving their pay behind. They would get jobs ashore and live at the runner's boardinghouse, which would somehow get the bulk of their pay. Meanwhile the ship from which they had deserted had finished loading, replaced the deserters with new men furnished by the very combine which tempted the first sailors to desert. A bounty of fifty dollars per sailor was collected from the captain, besides one and perhaps two months' advance of the sailor's wages, to cover such indebtedness as the sailor was sure to have incurred to the boardinghouse. And so the process was repeated. Everybody profited by it but the sailor. The captain, or owners, pocketed the wages the deserting sailor had forfeited, the boardinghouse shark pocketed the bounty and the advances in wages, and Jack held the bag.

As we approached the harbor of Tacoma, the motor launch cast off, the runner shouting that he would be waiting on the dock. In a short time we reached our anchorage, cast off the tug, and dropped anchor. Tacoma harbor was crowded with ships of all kinds, and her waterfront seemed a forest of masts. There were big three- and four-masted coastwise lumber schooners, three- and four-masted barques and full-rigged ships loading wheat and lumber for all corners of the world.

We stayed at anchor for several days until a berth along the dock was vacated, then a tug assisted us in. As we approached the dock, there was the crimp, a reception committee of one, all ready to reap the harvest he had sown a few days previous. We had hardly moored the ship and put the gangplank over, when he came aboard, hail fellow well met with all of us, and made a beeline for the focs'le, his pockets bulging with cigars, cigarettes and half pints of whiskey.

After the work on deck was finished, the sailors drifted back to the focs'le to find the crimp comfortably at home, affability itself, and handing out smokes and drinks to everybody. One swig of whiskey was all that was needed to make the picture he painted in our mind's eye even brighter. It didn't take much to make even the dullest among us see the difference between a dark, cheerless focs'le and the bright lights of a honky-tonk, between struggling on an ice-sheathed yard with a stubborn sail on a wintry night and sitting in the corner of a bar with a complaisant houri by one's side, between washing salt beef and beans down with black tea and savoring a juicy steak. No more maggoty ships' biscuits, stagnant drinking water, no more lookouts at night or turns at the wheel, a two-hour exposure to a biting, searching wind, or driving rain and spindrift. Liverpool Jack, a Norwegian and one of the Swedes were already busy packing their bags. Others were wavering, and the discussion had become rather noisy when it was interrupted by the arrival of a newcomer.

Into the focs'le stepped a very attractive young woman. She was one of two ladies who conducted a Seaman's Mission, and she had come, as she did to every ship arriving in Tacoma, to invite us all up to the

Mission. She produced some tracts which she handed around, smiling sweetly at everybody, and ignoring the sarcastic remarks of the crimp, who knew her as a doughty antagonist in their constant struggle for the souls of sailors. Against the promises of the fleshpots of Egypt held out by the crimp all she could offer was a get-together to sing hymns, have coffee and cake, play games like pool and dominoes, and reading matter. We took the tracts and promised to come to the Mission. Then she departed with a smile for everybody, leaving the field to the crimp, who tried his best to counteract the effect her charm had had on us, but who found it useless for the time being to try to add any more of us to the three who were ready to follow him.

Liverpool Jack went aft on the scant chance that the captain might pay him off, but it was a useless errand, and the three deserters went down the gangplank in full view of the mate and voicing some choice obscene epithets for the benefit of anybody aft that might be watching their departure. I couldn't resist the temptation to shoot a few parting barbs into Liverpool Jack, and he turned on me a flood of billingsgate. "You wait, you dirty Dutch bastard. I'll get you before you get out of this town," were his parting words, but we never met again.

The Russian carpenter also left the ship carrying his bag on his shoulder, and we helped him with his tool chest down onto the dock. Nobody attempted to interfere. The ship had no need of sailors until ready to go to sea again, and replacements were abundant.

One day a photographer from Seattle came aboard. He made a specialty of photographing ships coming up Puget Sound, in Tacoma and Seattle harbors, and group pictures of crews. He received permission from the captain to take a picture of our crew, and we all grouped ourselves around the mainmast. Most ships had a painting of the vessel hanging in the captain's salon, which the photographer was usually given permission to photograph. From the negative he made prints which he sold to the crew. The *Gwydyr Castle* had no such painting, much to his disappointment, but the mate told him there was a Dutchman called Bismarck in the focs'le, who was always messing around with water colors. Perhaps he could paint a picture of the *Gwydyr Castle*. I was pointed out to him, and told him, sure I could make him a picture of the ship under full sail, if he could get me a sheet of water-color paper, and the captain would let me have a day off.

The captain gave me the next day off, and the photographer came back the same afternoon with the paper; so the next morning I started in, standing on the settee running all around the lower bunks, with the paper propped up in my bunk, the porthole furnishing the light. I became so absorbed in my work that I didn't even take time off for the midday meal, and by evening it was finished. What the picture lacked as a work of art, it made up for in accuracy of detail, and my shipmates thought it grand, an opinion in which I fully concurred. The next morning the photographer returned and was delighted too. He took the picture back to Seattle with him and returned a few days later with prints of the picture and the group photograph. He charged a dollar apiece for the prints and they went like hot cakes. Everybody, including myself, bought a photograph. I even shelled out two dollars for one of each, and also let the photographer keep the original.

I was so proud of my success that it never occurred to me that the photographer had used me as an easy mark.

He evidently thought I was too good a thing not to be made use of further, for he took me aside and tried to convince me I didn't belong in a ship's focs'le. He wanted me to quit the ship and work for him. Why I didn't avail myself of the opportunity to settle in America, with a ready-made job, I don't know to this day, unless I wasn't yet ready to settle down, and the thought that I might settle in America hadn't occurred to me. In spite of its rigors and hardships, the life of a deep-water sailor appealed to me still. It was colorful, and I was under obligation to no one. Through it I had become hardened both physically and mentally. The photographer was very much surprised when I said no to his proposal, and looking back over the years I have often wondered what would have happened to me if I had accepted and settled in Seattle in 1902.

We had shore leave every night, and after supper, except for the night watchman on deck, the ship was deserted, and the men scattered all over town. The only money we had was a dollar a week, which the skipper allowed us to draw against our wages. He didn't care if we jumped ship, as long as we left our wages behind. Legally we weren't entitled to our wages until the end of the three years for which we had signed on.

There was a boisterous red-light district in Tacoma, whose clientele was composed of lumberjacks and sailors, attracted like moths to the brassy dance halls, gin mills, and a long, narrow street where prostitutes of all races exhibited their dubious charms in show windows. A few of the crew, like myself, were not drinking men and we got in the habit of going up to the Sailor's Mission every evening. There was always a surprisingly large number of sailors sitting around, reading, playing pool or checkers. One of the main attractions of the place was a collection of thousands of photographs of ships and crews which had come into Tacoma. The crew pictures especially were examined by the men for former shipmates.

The mission was run by two ladies, one in her early twenties and very pretty. Their charm and kindness were the main factors in the Mission's success. The main room contained a parlor organ, and when the ladies discovered I could play the piano, I became somewhat of a privileged character. Sunday afternoons were always devoted to a hymn-singing session followed by a generous repast of coffee and cake. I would take my seat at the organ, and the two ladies led the aggregation of sailors to the strains of "Where Is My Wandering Boy Tonight?" or "Lead Kindly Light," and other hymns.

Those two ladies did a wonderful work, and thousands of sailors must hold them in grateful memory. They knew all about the traffic in sailors, and did as much as they could to combat it by warning the sailors how it actually worked.

In spite of the crimp's repeated visits to our focs'le no more sailors deserted, but six men were missing from our original crew—poor Tim and the old sailmaker, dead, the Russian carpenter, and the three who had followed the lure of the crimp. I ran across the Russian carpenter one evening. He was glad to see me, and he invited me into a bar to have a beer. He had found a good job ashore as a carpenter, and was through with the sea for good. He meant to settle down in America and become a citizen. The others I never saw again.

By the time the crimp came aboard for the last time we were pretty fed up with him, and his freehandedness with cigars and liquor got him nowhere. I began to kid him unmercifully, and it seemed to get under his skin. So much so that he threatened to get even with me somehow. Luckily I never ran into him ashore, for I might have been in for a rough time.

The ship finally had her full cargo, and the next morning we were to leave the dock and anchor out in the harbor. That evening I went up to the Mission for the last time, to say good-by to the two ladies. We sat down to coffee and cake, and they asked me to keep in touch with them, which I promised, and did for a year or so, until the rush of new events and impressions absorbed me. But I have never forgotten them.

Years afterwards, I was asked to write a sketch for the "Keeping Posted" column of the *Saturday Evening Post*, and I told of my experiences in Tacoma. When it was published, I received a letter from one of the ladies, by then retired, recalling my visits to them. At the same time I received a large photograph of the *Gwydyr Castle* sailing up Puget Sound, sent to me by the president of a contracting and bridge-building concern, who had a large collection of photographs of sailing ships arriving in Puget Sound.

When morning came we got ready to leave the dock. While we were waiting for the tug, who should appear on the wharf but the crimp? He began to ridicule us for saps who didn't know enough to come in out of the wet. I talked back to him in the same tone, telling him exactly what I thought of him and his kind. Then he began to threaten to see to it that we should get three hard cases aboard to replace the three sailors who had deserted. We assured him we would be ready to receive his hard cases, and see whether we couldn't soften them up. The hawsers were thrown off the bollards and the ship edged away from the wharf, but his gibes rang in our ears until we were out of earshot.

Out in the harbor, and out of the way of shipping, we dropped anchor, waiting only for the new hands to come aboard, to start on our voyage to Callao. The first of the new hands arrived that afternoon. The bosun appeared in the focs'le door, in his tow a young fellow carrying two paper suitcases. We were sitting around the focs'le as the bewildered-looking lad, in store clothes, stepped in. He was a big flabby-looking fellow. At first we thought he was a peddler, and waited for him to open his suitcases and show his wares, but when he just stood there, looking lost, it dawned on us that he might be a new hand. He seemed to have no idea of what his next move should be. Finally we questioned him and discovered that he had meant to enlist in the Navy, inspired by the heroic account of the United States Navy's activities in the Spanish American war. He came from Spokane in the State of Washington, and had been told the best way to go about it was to go to Seattle. There he fell into the hands of a man who told him just to leave everything to him. He would see that he got into the Navy. Today he had been conveyed to Tacoma to board his ship. On the launch, on the way out to our ship, doubts had begun to assail him. He had seen plenty of pictures of warships, and the *Gwydyr Castle* didn't look like any of them; but the man said he couldn't get on a battleship at first, this was a training ship. All the boys enlisting in the Navy had to go on a training ship at first.

When we disillusioned him, it was too late to do anything about it. There he was, signed on as an able-bodied seaman, and bound for Callao. He had never

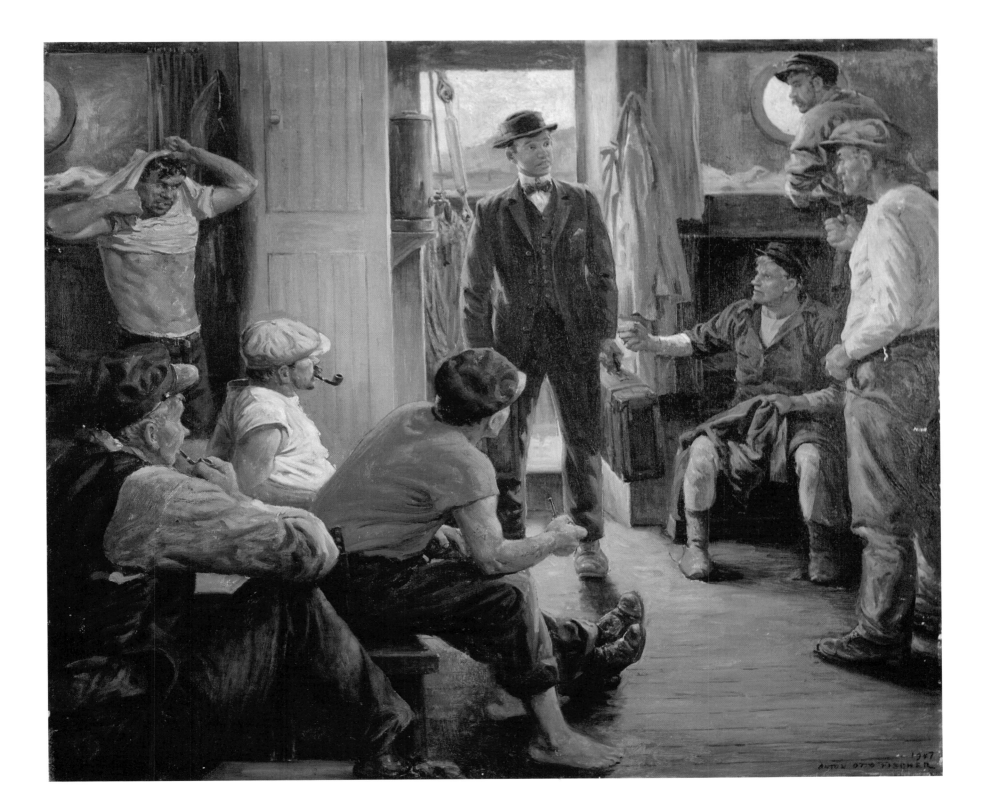

been near the water, and proved completely useless. He was seasick most of the time, and no amount of coercion could make him go aloft. I couldn't help but feel sympathetic towards him, remembering my terrible initiation into seafaring life aboard the *Renskea*. He became permanent "Peggy," and had to keep the focs'le clean, trim and fill the kerosene lamp, and perform all the menial chores. The only thing he ever did on deck was to join us in tailing onto a halyard or brace. Fortunately the focs'le crowd was good-natured, and he was never subject to abuse, though all sorts of practical jokes were played upon him.

The next day a launch came alongside, and up the Jacob's ladder came three tough-looking hombres, followed by an even tougher individual. The latter was short and powerfully built, with only one eye, and had a cartridge belt and six-shooter strapped around his middle. While the three sailors' seabags were handed up to them, he walked over to the mate and told him he was staying aboard until the ship got under way; that the mate would be responsible for the presence of the three newcomers on board from six in the morning until six at night and he, the one-eyed man, would stand guard from six in the evening until six in the morning. He was the insurance that they would be on board when the *Gwydyr Castle* got under way, and he wasn't taking any chances that they might swim ashore. They represented one hundred and fifty dollars in bounty, or, as we called it, blood money, plus whatever advance in wages the captain had been persuaded to pay.

The three new hands went forward to the focs'le, and it seemed as though the crimp had done his best to carry out his threat. They looked and talked like hard cases. Their unkempt appearance and bloodshot eyes gave proof that they had been on a prolonged bout of dissipation, and they looked really worse than they were. One was a loud-mouthed Norwegian, over six feet tall, with a week's growth of stubby blond beard, and who looked like a potential bully. The second was a shifty-looking Swede. The last was a rather goodlooking German in spite of his dissipated appearance, and the foulest-mouthed man I had ever met. He couldn't open his mouth without cloaking anything that came out with smut and obscenity. But they looked like good sailors, and such they proved to be when we once put to sea, and the effects of their dissipation wore off.

Both the Swede and the German had venereal disease. They made no attempt to hide the fact, rather they boasted about it. They got what was left of the bunks, the two least desirable, and wanted to know all about the ship and her officers. We told them work was fairly easy, but the food terrible, though we were to take on new provisions in Tacoma, and we had great hopes that provisions procured in America would be of better quality. However, the steward was the meanest son of a bitch afloat and there was no telling what he would try to put over on us.

"Peggy" brought in the chow, and they loosened up about themselves. Their experiences corroborated everything we had heard of the traffic in sailors around Puget Sound. They had deserted from various ships, and worked in the sawmills for a while, soon only to get in trouble again—the Norwegian and Swede through drink, the German through women; and here they were, back on a limejuicer. They felt almost like convicts, with the one-eyed watchman pacing back and forth on deck in front of the focs'le, his six-shooter plainly displayed.

Later in the day the water boat came alongside to replenish our supply of fresh water, and was followed shortly by a barge loaded with barrels, tubs and bags, our new provisions. When we unloaded them and stowed them aft our hopes ran high. There were new-looking barrels of salt beef and pork, tub after tub labeled plum, apricot, crab apple, evidently jam to replace the inevitable orange marmalade, tubs of margarine, boxes of hardtack, cases of canned beef and bags of dried beans and peas. It looked as though we would at last have food fit for a man to eat.

Towards evening everything had been taken aboard and the *Gwydyr Castle* was ready to start out the next morning. There was no more shore leave. The captain arrived aboard around midnight, and early in the morning a tug came alongside. We manned the capstan, heaving up the anchor, took the tug's hawser, and in a short while Tacoma harbor disappeared in the morning mist. Once off Port Townsend, the wind being fresh and fair, we cast off from the tug, which turned to come alongside and take off the one-eyed guard. The sails were hoisted and sheeted home and towards late afternoon we passed Cape Flattery where we shaped our course southeastwards towards Callao.

In a few days all signs of our stay in port had been removed, and we settled down to the old routine. The skipper had been able to ship another carpenter and sailmaker, and the three new hands proved themselves to be capable sailors. The boy from Spokane was of course only excess baggage, and the starboard-watch was sore when he was assigned to it because somebody always had to double up when it came his turn at the wheel. The big Norwegian too was in the starboard-watch, and he took to bullying the lad. It took a little

time to adjust the relations of the newcomers to the old crew. The Norwegian started to assume a rather overbearing attitude, but a succession of near accidents cooled him off. Several times tackle came down from above, barely missing him, and once a marlinspike came hurtling down from aloft, burying its quivering length in the deck close by his feet. He would rave, shout and threaten, but accidents will happen.

During one dog-watch he was definitely put in his place. He didn't like his bunk, and thought that he was entitled to the one occupied by the Spokane boy. With all his shortcomings, we liked the boy better than the loud-mouthed Norwegian, or, more accurately, no one disliked the boy. When we saw that the lad was overawed by the big fellow's bluster and was ready to give up his bunk, we objected. It ended when Fatty Ecklund told the Norwegian to put up or shut up, and he declined the issue. That was the end of his attempts to bully, and in the course of time he became a good shipmate.

None of us ever took much to either the Swede or the German. We didn't like living in close intimacy with the "clapp." As hard cases, all three of them were false alarms. Before they ever came aboard, we had discussed the crimp's threat, and had decided to gang up on any one or all three of them if they tried to be nasty.

We had fair sailing all the way down the coast with the usual spell of calm and variable airs off the equator, but after about ten days of aimless drifting, we got a fair slant of wind, and were soon on our way again.

For a few days after leaving Puget Sound we had fresh meat and potatoes. We knew that sooner or later the regular provisions taken on at Tacoma would be given us, but our expectations were high this time.

THE GRIEVANCE COMMITTEE

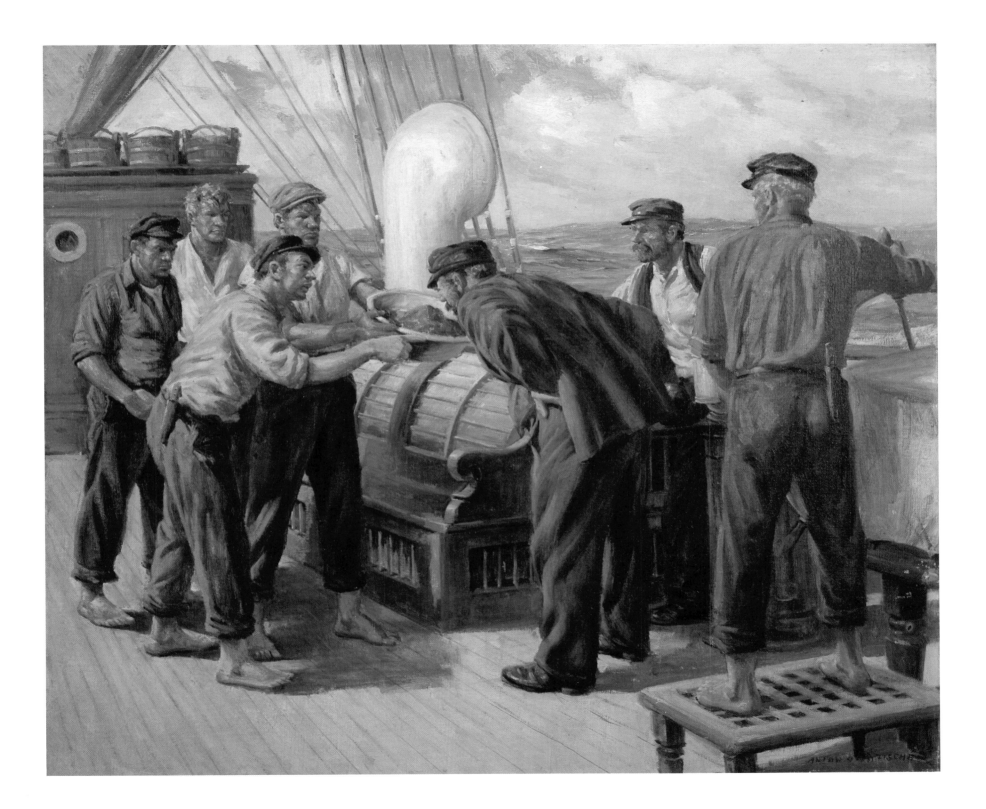

That made our disappointment even greater when the first piece of salt pork came from the galley. We looked in consternation at the small chunk of it in the dishpan, and went to see the cook about it. He protested there was nothing he could do. He had cooked the big chunk "Peggy" had gotten from the steward, but it was so fat, it had cooked down to less than half its size. When the salt beef appeared the next day, we hit the ceiling. It was a curious magenta color, and when "Peggy" tried to divide it, his knife made no impression. It would have taken an ax to have cut it into pieces. We stared at it, wondering from what animal it came, for beef it certainly was not. Perhaps it was horsemeat. It looked exactly like a colored chunk of wood and was of about the same consistency, without the slightest trace of fat or gristle. One of the fellows suggested it might be elephant's meat. Some elephant might have died in a zoo and its meat been corned. We were ready to murder the steward, and cursed ourselves for fools at not having left the ship in Tacoma. I took the meat, and with my sheath-knife whittled a ship's model out of the chunk.

When a few days later our menu called again for salt beef and beans, and the same wooden chunk came from the galley, we decided to do something about it. Led by the big Norwegian, we trooped aft to the poop, where the captain sat on the skylight, his game leg stretched out in front of him on a pillow. We walked up, and asked him whether he thought the beef was fit for a man to eat. He didn't like our unceremonious intrusion on his privacy, but he got up and put his nose in the dishpan, remarking that it smelled all right, and what did we think was the matter with it? We were so mad, we lost all sense of awe and respect for the old man, and among other things told him that it was so tough no one could cut it, let alone eat it. To prove our point, I produced the ship's model I had whittled from the first piece, and held it out to him.

He called the steward up to the poop and asked him about it, but the steward protested that he had bought *bona fide* provisions, and it wasn't his fault. Seeing the steward there made us all see red and we recited a litany of all the scurvy tricks he had played on us, illuminated by all the names we could think of to call him. We left the poop when the captain finally asserted his authority and ordered us forward, but not before again voicing our opinions of the ship, its owners, and the whole gang aft.

We were in a mutinous mood. The ship's biscuits or hardtack looked beautiful. They were a snowy white color, but when dropped into a pannikin of coffee, they sank immediately to the bottom, and never softened. The margarine was lumpy and had an iridescent sheen. Some of the fellows swore they had seen better grease used in the launching of ships. The tubs with their gaudy labels of plum, apricot and crab apple, contained nothing but the most inferior grade of crab-apple jam, full of the pips and cores. We had a feeling that we had been sold down the river, everything was so far below even the low standard of the *Gwydyr Castle*. Fortunately the canned beef was good, as was the flour, but our biggest gripe was the hardtack. That was the only thing in abundance with which we could appease our hunger, and when we replenished the hardtack box in the focs'le for the first time with the new supply, and found it almost inedible, our rage was mutinous. The old hardtack had looked less appetizing, and was full of weevils, but at least, when dropped into a pannikin of hot coffee or tea, it softened and was palatable. However,

mutinies at sea were rare and unprofitable occurrences.

The Swede who had joined the ship in Tacoma had amongst his effects a small oblong of dried india ink and since there was an "artist" in the focs'le, some of them wanted me to tattoo figures and ships on their arms and chests. We had no needle, but I found a sharp steel pen and one dog-watch I started in tattooing a full rigged ship on Fatty Ecklund's chest. It must have hurt, but he stood it like a trooper, and both he and I were very proud of the result. After the success of that first attempt, I was called upon frequently, and decorated a few arms with anchors, stars and flags. My prize effort, though, was when I tattooed a naked *houri* onto a fellow's bicep, so that when he flexed his muscles, she did a sort of hootchie-kootchie dance.

The voyage down to Callao was without incidents. We picked up a fair wind south of the equator, and soon we arrived at our destination, and dropped anchor in the harbor off Callao.

CHAPTER

6

CALLAO TO YONKERS

O**N ARRIVING** in Callao we remained at anchor for several days before we moved to a dock to discharge our cargo. While the crew was busy making things shipshape aloft, the captain and the steward were rowed ashore in the gig, and in a short while the steward returned with fresh meat and potatoes.

Once we were moored to the dock, evenings and nights were ours to spend as we chose, and we went ashore, exploring the sections of Callao which offered the best opportunities for the sort of diversion sailors looked for. The Callao waterfront was full of such opportunities, and it never took long to separate the fellows from the little money a pennypinching skipper allowed them to draw against their wages.

We always went ashore in a group; partly for companionship and partly for protection, as street fights and bar-room brawls were a nightly occurrence in Callao's red-light district. It took very little liquor to make the sailors noisy and sometimes quarrelsome. I never drank very much and several times became involved in fisticuffs shepherding a gang of drunken shipmates back aboard the ship.

With many people the terms "drunkenness" and "sailors" were synonymous, when, as a matter of fact, deep-water sailors were by force of circumstance more abstemious than any other class of workers. A gang of sailors would come down the street roaring and shouting and people would give them a wide berth with a shrug of the shoulders. They were just another bunch of drunken sailors to them, oblivious of the fact that those men had probably just finished a three- or four-month voyage of enforced abstemiousness and leading a life in many ways abnormal to lusty men in the prime of life. Day after day the same deadly monotony, eating coarse food, too often of doubtful quality, cooped up in a focs'le with men of all types, both good fellows and degenerates, and the total absence of feminine companionship. It all led naturally to the red-light districts of the ports where their need for gaiety, laughter, music and women could be satisfied cheaply. Only a drink or two was necessary to set them going. They had to go back to the same severe and almost ascetic existence, cherishing only the memory of the last fling ashore and the anticipation of the next one to come. No wonder the sailors went ashore to buy all the pleasures they could with what few dollars, shillings or pesos they had in their pockets.

There were of course the Seaman's Missions, but as a general rule the fellows had to be pretty well broke before they went to enjoy the innocent diversions offered at such institutions. The Mission at Tacoma was the best I ever ran across, and that was due largely to the two ladies who ran it. They had a genuine and sympathetic understanding of that queer character, the deep-water sailor.

Among the dozen or so square-rigged ships then anchored in Callao, was a big German four-masted, full-rigged ship. We met some of her crew in one of the waterfront drinking places, and compared notes as to food, officers, work, etc. The accounts of the food they got made our mouths water. When I expressed the opinion that they were bragging, they offered to prove it, and invited me to come aboard and have a meal the next day.

Their ship was a revelation to me. It was immaculate, paint and brass work shining, every rope carefully coiled. I suspected, even before I was told, that the discipline was of an almost naval standard. She was a big ship, carrying forty-five men altogether, and I couldn't help comparing her with our *Gwydyr Castle* and her polyglot, roughneck crew. The German carried three ordinary seamen and two deck boys in the focs'le as well as the able-bodied seamen, and the lines were distinctly drawn. The A.B.'s lorded it over the ordinary seamen, and they in turn over the deck boys. On the *Gwydyr Castle* we had no such distinctions. On our ship "Peggy" performed the menial tasks assigned to the deck boys on the German ship, and we all took turns at being "Peggy."

My eyes popped when supper was brought in. There was variety and it was well cooked. Even at sea besides the usual salt beef and pork they received a variety of canned meats and vegetables, and soft bread every day. The *Gwydyr Castle* was a poorhouse in comparison. However, the German captain and officers were martinets, and there was none of the comparatively easy-going atmosphere of our ship.

The boy from Spokane left the ship in Callao. His story had become known to the captain, and to his credit, he took steps to have the boy repatriated. After seeing the American consul, the captain got in touch with the boy's parents, and arrangements were made for the lad to leave on the next steamer going north. His departure was no loss to us, but we all wished him good luck.

One day an American battleship arrived in the harbor. It was the *U.S.S. Kearsarge.* As there was also a British man-of-war in port, we expected some fireworks when the crews of both ships met on shore, and we weren't disappointed. It started with a fist fight in a saloon and soon became a general roughhouse. As the news spread along the waterfront, American and British sailors rushed to the scene from all directions, and a first-class riot developed. When the police arrived to put a stop to it, both factions turned on them, and the disturbance wasn't quelled until the small hours of the morning. Some of our fellows had been mixed up in the affair, and returned to the ship somewhat the worse for wear. There was never any lack of excitement in Callao, if one was inclined to look for it.

It didn't take long to discharge our cargo of wheat, and we moved out into the bay again, where we anchored. Word went around that we were to pick up a cargo of sugar along the Peruvian coast, and then sail back around the Horn to the Delaware Breakwater. Late one afternoon the captain returned from shore, bringing with him a new hand to replace the Spokane boy. His name was Jack Williams and he came from Boston. Beyond the clothes on his back he had nothing, no sea bag or bundle. His previous ship had been wrecked off the River Plate and he and three other sailors had drifted in an open boat for ten days, before they were seen by a passing ship and picked up. The rescue ship had landed them in Callao, and he had been on the beach ever since. At one time in his career he had been a prize fighter, and a tap dancer in vaudeville, and in Callao had eked out a living by performing in waterfront dives, until he was signed on by our captain.

He was a real acquisition to the focs'le and soon became a favorite with everybody. He relieved the tedium of our existence with his dancing, and an inexhaustible supply of dialect stories, Irish, Yiddish, German and Negro. He was of medium height and compactly built, but as quick on his feet as a cat. He was very jolly and good-natured, but at the same time gave the impression that he could handle any two of us if he had to. His knowledge of seamanship was limited, but he caught on quickly.

The day after his arrival, the *Gwydyr Castle* got under way again. Evidently remembering our violent protest about the salt beef taken on in Tacoma, the steward bought other provisions in Callao, and they were of better quality, though as far as quantity was concerned, we never received an ounce more than was required by law.

We learned that our cargo of sugar was not to be taken on all at one place, but at five different places along the coast of Peru. At the first stop there was no harbor, and we anchored off shore in the Pacific swell. The sugar, packed in two-hundred-pound bags, was brought out to the ship by big surf boats. When the surf ran too high, the loading was abandoned until the sea moderated. We had to do all the lading and stowing ourselves and the hand winches were rigged again, reminiscent of Panama. The sugar bags were hoisted out of the surf boats and lowered into the hold. We utilized the first bags to erect a platform shoulder-high right under the open main hatch. Then bags were lowered onto the platform and from there shifted onto our backs, to be carried the length of the hold to wherever the mate and the bosun indicated. Carrying those two-hundred-pound bags was exhausting work, and when we stopped at six in the evening, we were dog-tired. The work shifted around so that we spent one day in the hold, and the next at the winches. As the ship was constantly rolling in the open roadstead, mishaps were quite frequent, and there were always some bags on deck that had become immersed in the brine, a molasses juice oozing from under them.

When the ship's heavy rolling made lading impossible, the captain used our enforced idleness by having us clean the ship's bottom as far as possible. By this time the bottom was very foul, and the ship's consequent loss of speed was quite noticeable. Looking over the side into the clear tropical water, we could see the scummy green growth waving from the underwater portion of her sides.

The dinghy and the gig were lowered and we got into them, armed with long-handled, three-cornered scrapers. We would be, say, on the port side waiting our chance. When the ship took a deep roll to starboard, exposing the lower part of her hull to port we got to work with our scrapers, removing as much of the seaweed and barnacles as we could until she came rolling back to port again. We hated the job and much preferred wrestling with the heavy bags of sugar. There was a certain amount of danger in the operation, in that the small boats might be swamped by the return roll of the vessel, and we groused among ourselves because we felt that the little we could accomplish under such makeshift conditions, hardly justified the risk involved.

It was after the gig was almost swamped that we accidentally discovered a way to put a stop to the whole proceeding. We were scraping furiously at the exposed lower hull when the ship began to roll back. One of the sailors kept on scraping 'til the last moment, when the protruding edge of one of the ship's plates caught the scraper and jerked it from his hands. We watched the scraper sink down to the bottom through the clear water. Soon the mate received so many calls for scrapers, that his supply became exhausted and the work had to be abandoned. We had never heard of such a word as "sabotage," but we certainly worked on that principle. Both the captain and the mate were furious at what they suspected was chicanery on our part, but there was no way of proving anything.

We stopped at three more points along the coast, in every case anchoring in the roadstead beyond the surf. The conditions were always the same, though the rolling became less as the ship, with each additional load, lay deeper in the water. We had naturally no shore leave, and fresh food was unobtainable, so we were back on our salt beef and pork regime, relieved by an occasional fish dinner, when we had been lucky enough to catch fish over the side.

The final stop, where we were to take on the bulk of our cargo, was a small settlement at the head of a landlocked harbor. We sailed through a narrow rocky inlet, and were greeted by the raucous barking of hundreds of sea lions sunning themselves on the rocks, and by flocks of pelicans. We anchored in quiet water, a half mile from the only strip of beach affording landing for a small boat. On one side of the cove were high rocks shutting out the sea, and also such breezes as might have given us relief from the almost unbearable heat. On the other side was a rocky shore, evidently a breeding place for sea lions. Just beyond the beach was a bungalow and a flagstaff flying the British flag. Farther inland, looking like a part of the landscape, was a group of low, thatched huts. A few homemade boats were pulled up on the beach, and a group of natives had gathered at the water's edge. A ship was a rare sight in the cove. There must have been a larger settlement or town farther inland, but we never saw it, or heard its name.

As soon as we dropped anchor, the skipper was rowed ashore by the apprentices to pay his respects at the bungalow. It was occupied by an Englishman and two ladies. He was the local agent, and transacted all business with such ships as might call.

The next morning barges laden with sugar came alongside and we resumed loading. The heat was oppressive and swimming in the evening was a welcome relief. At first it was disconcerting to have sea lions pop up amongst us, but they proved harmless, and there were no sharks, so the evening swim became a ritual.

One evening the captain returned from a day ashore, bringing with him a beachcomber. He was an American, well over six feet tall, but he was half-starved and his clothes mere rags. He was allowed to stay on board while we were taking on our cargo, and we fixed a makeshift berth for him in the sail locker as there was no room in the focs'le, but otherwise he was a member of the crew. We called him "Bo." He looked big enough to do the work of two men, but was so weakened by privation and near starvation that it was several days before he was of any use in the work of lading the ship. He came aboard during suppertime, and we were greatly amused when we offered him tea and hardtack. As the tea was poured into his pannikin, he politely repeated, "That's enough, that's enough," when the pannikin was three-quarters full, but kept following the spout of the teapot until his pannikin was overflowing. The first time he took his place by the platform in the hold to have a two-hundred-pound bag of sugar put on his back, he folded up like an accordion. He never recovered his strength while on board to be of much help, but he became a prime favorite with us just the same. He took our kidding good-naturedly and enlivened our evenings with tales of his adventures as a beachcomber. We were sorry to see him go when he was finally put ashore after we had our full cargo and were ready to put to sea again.

Our first Sunday in the harbor provided plenty of excitement. At eight bells (eight A.M.), the captain called for the gig, and was rowed ashore by the apprentices. He went off before we had a chance to ask for permission to go ashore. After breakfast some of us went aft to ask the mate whether we could lower one of the big lifeboats and row ashore. He said that the captain had left strict orders that under no circumstances were we to be allowed to use a boat, and that no shore leave was to be granted. We couldn't see why we should be denied permission to leave the ship for a few hours. All we could possibly do in that God-forsaken hole, was to walk around and get the feel of solid earth under our feet again. The mate was rather sympathetic, but he had his orders and couldn't go against them.

We went back to the focs'le a disgruntled outfit. None of the crew could see the justice of the captain's actions. While anchored off shore, shore leave was impossible, but here we were only half a mile away, and it didn't seem fair that after all those preceding weeks of hard work we should be denied the chance for a little diversion. Possibly the captain was afraid some of us would desert the ship, but no one in his right mind would think of jumping ship in such an impossible spot as that.

The more we discussed the matter, the sorer we got, and finally we decided we would go ashore anyhow, boat or no boat. They could prevent us from getting a boat over, but not from swimming ashore. We rigged a tackle from the foreyard and put a sling around the big tub used for washing down the deck. Then we took off our clothes and packed them in it, covering them with a tarpaulin. We then lowered the tub over the side. By this time the mate had become aware of what was going on, and began to remonstrate with us, but his words fell on deaf ears. A couple of planks were thrown overboard to assist the less efficient swimmers and, with the mate, the cook, the carpenter, the sailmaker, the bosun and the apprentices watching the proceedings, we jumped overboard, and laboriously made our way ashore. Birmingham was the only sailor who stayed behind. He couldn't swim, and was afraid to take the chance. The strongest swimmers amongst us pushed the tub, while others stayed behind, pushing the planks to which some of the poorer swimmers clung. We made slow progress, and a group of natives gathered to watch, among them quite a few women and girls who beat a hasty giggling retreat when they saw us emerge as naked as the Lord created us. As we approached shore the rocky bottom was covered with a sharp spiny growth, which broke off at the touch, and we spent a painful hour or so extracting the spines from each other's anatomy. We then hauled the tub and the planks up on the beach, got into our clothes and started out for the settlement, to explore its possibilities and look for some excitement.

There were hardly any signs of life as we strolled ankle deep in dust, along the road winding among thatched adobe huts. Here and there a child peeped out through a doorway, and a few emaciated dogs barked their resentment. On the outskirts of the settlement we came across a low-roofed hut, displaying a crude sign showing that it was a drinking place. We had no money amongst us, but we entered and began bartering for drinks. Our ignorance of Spanish was a handicap, but some of the fellows took off their shirts and offered them accompanied by a drinking motion, and the swarthy proprietor produced some of the vilest liquor I have ever tasted. One taste was all I wanted of that raw homemade firewater, but some of the gang imbibed quite freely, and in no time were feeling the effects. They became noisy and ready for any sort of deviltry. They showed an inclination to get nasty when the proprietor refused to serve them any more, and the sober ones amongst us had our hands full to get them out of the place. As our boisterous party made its way back to the village there wasn't a sign of life in the little settlement. We had quite a job preventing some of the

drunks from trying to enter huts in the search of amatory adventure. There might have been serious trouble if they had.

When we finally reached the beach again, we felt rather cheated. There was nothing to do. The beach was merely a hot strip of sand, no shade anywhere to escape from under the broiling sun, and all doors firmly closed against us. Then one of the drunks, a Swede, noticed the British flag flying from the staff in front of the agent's bungalow. He was for hauling it down, a proposal heartily endorsed by his companions in drink. Belligerently opposing any of the others' attempts to stop them from committing the outrage, they lurched over to the yard and hauled down the flag, unknotted the halyards, and in its place up went the greasy cloth cap of one of the sailors, while two frightened ladies watched in consternation from behind the windows.

When the drunks came back to us lying on the beach, we were rather tired of the whole episode. It seemed a long distance out to the ship, with a half dozen of us drunk. It was unlikely that we could negotiate the distance, towing and pushing the tub and the planks as well. We tried to attract the attention of the men aboard ship, but if the mate saw or heard he paid no attention. He was going to let us stew in the juice of our own making. Towards late afternoon when the high cliff at the western side of the cove threw its shadow over the water, a conveyance pulled up at the bungalow, and out stepped the agent and the captain, and immediately the gig left the ship for the shore. On reaching the beach the captain hobbled over to where we were grouped on the beach, with the drunks stretched out on the sand sleeping it off. He was thoroughly mad, and wanted to know who had given us permission to leave the ship, and how we had gotten ashore. We told him no one had given permission, the mate had refused us a boat and we had swum ashore. And we didn't need his Goddamn boat to get back either. We could swim back again.

By this time the gig had landed on the beach, and he ordered as many of us as it would hold to get in. We roused up the drunks, and put them into the boat which pushed off and returned to the ship. The captain said it would return for the rest of us and the tub, but without waiting we stripped, packed our clothes in the tub again, and started our return swim to the *Gwydyr Castle.*

Somehow it seemed twice as long and hard, and when the gig came back most of the boys were glad to climb into it. Two of the sailors and myself remained stubborn however and continued to swim. The gig took the tub in tow, and we reached the vessel even before it.

The whole incident simply highlighted the bad feeling between the afterguard and the men in the focs'le. Loyalty towards their ship was almost automatic with most deep-water sailors. Ashore, discussing their ships with other sailors, they always stressed their merits and resented any belittling remarks, but the crew of the *Gwydyr Castle* was only too aware that they were merely part of the overhead in running the ship, to be carried as cheaply as the law allowed. We never saw any evidence that our well-being was considered to be of any importance, and it was only due to lack of popular leadership among us that we did not break out in open mutiny. The day after our escapade we resumed lading, and in a few days the last sling of sugar bags came aboard.

In Callao the steward had neglected to replenish our supply of fresh water, either through oversight or, as we suspected, because he hoped he could do so without cost somewhere along the coast. About a mile beyond the settlement was a fresh-water lagoon, stagnant, and slightly brackish to taste. One morning we put some hogsheads over the side and towed them ashore with the gig and the dinghy. A cart took them to the lagoon where we filled them with the water dipped from the lagoon. They were then carted back to the beach and towed out to the ship. The operation took two days. The water was really unfit to drink. It was opaque in color, and as the voyage progressed it became filled with all sorts of wriggling larvae. One more black mark was chalked up against the steward. We raised such a kick about it that the cook was ordered to boil every drop issued for drinking.

It has always puzzled me why the biggest maritime nation, Britain, treated their sailing ship crews so stingily. If the *Gwydyr Castle* had been an isolated case, it might have been just our bad luck at shipping on her, but comparing notes with other crews in the ports visited, we found the complaints about the quantity and quality of the food universal. The turnover among the crews of limejuicers was constant. At every port sailors deserted, leaving their pay behind, and a captain of a Nova Scotian line, infamous amongst sailors all over the world, was heard to make the drunken boast in a café in Rio de Janeiro that in twenty years he had never paid off a man. On that particular ship the sailors were treated so badly, they would always desert the ship the first port reached, to be replaced by bums and drunks picked up along the waterfront, who were whipped into shape after the vessel was on the high seas. They in turn deserted, and so it went on, keeping the labor costs down to a minimum. On that ship it was a combination of bad food and sadistic bucco-officers. On the *Gwydyr Castle* we were at least spared the latter.

While we were in Tacoma, a full-rigged ship of the same Nova Scotian line arrived in port and a few days after arrival a United States marshal went aboard and a legal paper was fastened to her mainmast. The Norwegian Consulate had brought suit for damages against the line on behalf of a Norwegian sailor, a member of her crew. When the ship was only a few hours sailing out from Shanghai, the man had fallen from aloft. His fall had been broken enough by running gear to save his life, but he had suffered internal injuries and both his legs were broken. The captain had refused to return to Shanghai to put the man in a hospital, and had set the bones himself. When the ship arrived in Tacoma, the man was in bad shape. Both legs had to be rebroken and there wasn't a sailor in Tacoma who didn't hope the line would have to pay heavy damages. If the matter had been left to the sailors, it might have gone badly with that particular blue-nose captain.

I know of another case, from personal experience, that happened in New York City. A big four-masted ship was lying off Bayonne, New Jersey, laden with case oil for Shanghai. There seemed to be some difficulty in getting sailors to sign on for that particular voyage, or perhaps on that particular ship. She had half her crew but couldn't sail without her full complement. I had been paid off from the *Gwydyr Castle* and was staying at an Episcopal Seaman's Mission in Market Street. A group of us were sitting around the main room, when a man entered, saying that he was looking for ten men who would sign articles for a voyage to China and back. None of us were interested at all, and then he explained (handing out cigars) that he didn't want *bona fide* signatures. We could sign any name we wanted to, just so that the ship's articles were filled out

to the satisfaction of the port authorities, and the ship could get her clearance papers.

After some persuasion, backed up by the display of a roll of dollar bills, ten men followed him to an office on Cherry Street, where they signed ship's articles under fictitious names. That night the crimps got busy along Cherry and South Streets and picked up ten drunks who were taken over to Bayonne and put aboard the four-master. In the morning a tug came alongside and a gang of riggers from a Brooklyn shipyard came aboard. The tug got a hawser aboard and the riggers put the ship under sail. Once well beyond Sandy Hook the tug took the riggers off, and the ship was on its way around Cape Horn to China with half its crew shanghaied and leaving it up to the disgusted mates to whip the misfits into shape.

After the fresh water was taken aboard, the *Gwydyr Castle* was ready to put to sea again, but to get out of the harbor proved more difficult than anticipated. On entering the narrow, rocky inlet we had been favored by a fair slant of wind, but tacking against the same wind in that confined space was something else. The entrance, now the exit, was too narrow to permit much maneuvering in tacking, and day after day we were forced to abandon the attempt and return to our anchorage. We were all fed up with that place, and the daily frustration trying to get out was almost too much. Our tempers were getting short, and it involved me indirectly in another altercation.

During our swim ashore that Sunday morning, the German we had taken on in Tacoma had gotten a good dose of that spiney growth on the submerged rocks. None of the rest of us had suffered any after-effect, but his leg became infected, and he was incapacitated for about a week.

We had just returned to our anchorage after another unsuccessful attempt to negotiate the passage, when "Peggy" brought the chow to the focs'le. During the meal an argument arose, in the course of which the German called me a vile name. I lost my temper and threw my plate of peasoup in his face. He went for me, and we grappled on the focs'le floor, but were separated and pushed out on deck to finish our fight there. It was a blistering hot day and there were big blobs of the marine glue boiling up out of the deck seams. We squared off, and I threw a left at his chin. It seemed to stiffen him, and I followed immediately with another left which spun him clear around and he fell full-length on deck. He was completely out, and while I stood there panting a pool of blood began to form around his feet. I got scared, and then we saw what had happened. When we squared off he must have stood directly on one of the bubbles of glue. When my second blow spun him around the sole of his foot was glued to the deck, and a piece of skin the size of a silver dollar was torn loose. Hitting the deck his head barely missed a deck bolt, or I might have been in real trouble.

Finally one day, after over a week of failures, the wind slanted fair enough to enable us to sail out of the passage amid the barking of the sea lions. A fair, westerly wind stayed with us and we shaped our course south towards Cape Horn. We had an easy run down to fifty degrees south, where the winds began to freshen, and the Pacific swells grew bigger. However, we made fairly good time in spite of the ship's foul bottom, and soon were heading east. We had enjoyed fine sunny weather all along the coast, but now the skies became overcast and the falling barometer gave forecasts of dirty weather ahead. The light sails were taken in, and soon the ship was scudding before a heavy gale under only foresail and lower topsails. A tremendous sea rose, and steering became difficult. After the kicking wheel had lifted Birmingham clear off his feet and draped him over the wheelbox, injuring his side against the bronze bell fastened on top of the wheelbox, two men were stationed at the wheel. The ship acted like a roller coaster, being swept up to the heights on the crest of a huge wave and then swooping down into its deep valley. It was an awesome sight to look back and see a big sea forming astern, rearing up, up, up, until its monstrous mass towered above the stern, its translucent, bottle-green top heralding the coming crash of a breaking sea. After the ship had "pooped" a big sea, which threatened to wash the men at the wheel away, they were secured with ropes tied around their waists, and warned not to look back. However, we had the gale dead astern, and as though to make amends for those two hellish months rounding the Horn on our westerly voyage, this time we were carried east around the Horn in twenty-four hours.

Once around, the course was shaped northeast, and soon we picked up the southeast trade winds which carried us without interruption to the region of the equatorial doldrums. Our bad luck seemed to have run out, for we missed the expected becalming, and there was enough wind to carry us out of the doldrums in a short time. We picked up a steady easterly wind and set our course for the Atlantic seaboard, and the Delaware Breakwater in paticular.

The food situation had improved somewhat, due to the new supplies taken on in Callao. It was just as scanty and monotonous as ever, but at least what there was, was palatable. The drinking water, however, became worse every day, and we luxuriated on the few occasions when it rained, and we could fill every available receptacle with pure rain water. The cargo of sugar gave us an opportunity to add to our meager diet, and at the same time to get even, to some extent, with the parismoniousness of the steward, and the owners. We managed to get three of the two-hundred-pound bags out of the hold and into the focs'le, one bag at a time. The raids on the sugar were carefully planned, and it took both watches to accomplish them successfully.

Once at sea, the hatches were covered with tarpaulins and battened down. A raid on the sugar in daytime was impossible, and even at nighttime there was always the possibility that one of the mates would arrive at the scene of operations. We always chose a dark night. The fellows of the deck-watch would station themselves along the main deck, ready to give the prearranged warning signal if either of the mates seemed on the prowl. Meanwhile, the watch below worked furiously removing the tarpaulin and hatch cover. That done, a couple of sailors would descend into the hold and drag a bag to the hatch opening where the others were ready to hoist it on deck and transfer it to one of the lockers in the focs'le.

We repeated the operation three times during the voyage, and were never detected. It was brown granulated raw sugar, very rich in molasses content, and a welcome addition to our fare. We didn't dole it out. Every one could help himself to his heart's content, and we ate it almost like cereal. We derived much satisfaction too, when we pictured to ourselves what the skipper would say when he would find the sugar missing on unloading.

None of us knew the Delaware Breakwater, and when we asked the mate he said it was merely a port of call where we would get orders to sail to New York, Philadelphia or Boston. We were all looking forward to the end of our trip, and were determined to make some effort to get ourselves discharged. The fellows taken on in Tacoma, and Jack Williams, the American, could demand to be paid off, but we of the original crew had signed on for three years and could be held to it. We could always desert the ship, but our pay remained behind unless the captain saw fit to discharge us.

As we approached our destination, Jack Williams came into the focs'le one morning and roused us. The low-lying coast of Delaware was a faint smudge on the horizon, and by evening we dropped our anchor inside the breakwater. The captain was rowed ashore the next morning, and when he returned that evening we learned that we were to sail to New York and discharge our cargo at Yonkers.

A tug which had come down from New York with a tow of barges came alongside and offered to tow us up the Jersey coast to the anchorage off Staten Island for one hundred and fifty dollars. There was a lengthy palaver between the tugboat skipper and our captain, but as there was a fair wind blowing outside the captain refused the offer. At the most it would take only a few days to sail up the coast, and he didn't see why he should pay for towing, when he had sails and a crew to handle them.

On our arrival at the breakwater the steward had planned to go ashore for fresh provisions, but when orders were waiting to proceed to New York Harbor, he didn't think it worth while, although the ship's provisions were running low. We had looked forward to fresh

meat and potatoes, and when no efforts were made to get us some our morale hit a new low.

The next day we upped anchor, put sails on the ship and started up the coast towards Sandy Hook. As luck would have it, we ran into a pea-soup fog which blanketed the waters off the Jersey coast. The wind failed and we drifted on a glassy sea. We kept the foghorn going all the time and lookouts were doubled. Answering sirens and whistles came from all points of the compass. Steamers passed us so close we heard the swishing of their bow wave, and the voices of the men aboard, without seeing even a faint outline of the vessel itself. The thick weather lasted three days and when the fog finally cleared there wasn't much wind. The steward was scraping the bottoms of the last salt beef and pork barrels, and when our scanty rations were reduced, as a precaution, we were ready for murder. We refused to do work of any kind, except that necessary for sailing the ship. It was bloodless mutiny. The trip up the coast, which the captain had expected to make in three days, took ten. While becalmed in the thick weather and unable to maneuver, we were in constant danger of being run down, and it would have been a hundred and fifty dollars well invested if the captain had taken advantage of the tug skipper's offer. However, we finally passed Sandy Hook and entered lower New York Bay under a fair wind which enabled us to sail right up to the anchorage off Tottenville, Staten Island, where we had to await the coming of the quarantine officers.

No sooner had we dropped anchor, than a half dozen small boats pulled out from shore and came alongside. The tough-looking individuals aboard were boarding-house runners from the dives along South and Cherry Streets. Because we had not yet been through quarantine no one was allowed on board, but that didn't stop the crimps from carrying on their business alongside. We lined the rail and they passed up to us newspapers, cigarettes, cigars, pints of whiskey and cards printed with the names and addresses of their respective boardinghouses, each trying to exact our promises to come to his boardinghouse when we were paid off, as they confidently seemed to think we would be. They acted like a swarm of sharks around the carcass of a whale. Whether in Puget Sound or in New York Bay, they were all alike in their approach, trying to take advantage of the gullibility of the deep-water sailor, the easy mark.

When the quarantine officers appeared, the boats departed. After the official O.K. had been given to the ship and her crew, the captain and the steward went ashore. The steward's return was delayed for some reason or other, and we sat down at noon to the same old salt beef and beans, and a reduced portion at that. It was the last straw. When the bosun appeared in the focs'le door and called us out to make things shipshape on deck and aloft, we flatly refused. He left, but returned with the mate, who tried to enter the focs'le to reason with us. The big Norwegian threatened to throw him out on deck if he put his foot inside the focs'le, and realizing that we were ready for almost anything, he kept out. Standing outside the focs'le door, he continued reasoning with us, admitting that our resentment was justified. He finally persuaded us to go aloft and furl the sails which had been clewed up, and were hanging in their buntlines. The steward returned late in the afternoon, and when "Peggy" brought the supper we couldn't believe our eyes. Ham and eggs! Fresh bread and potatoes!

But better yet, word came from aft that anybody

who wanted could be paid off after the ship would be tied up at the dock in Yonkers. That sounded like a message from heaven, but we were soon to find out that there was a catch to it.

Next morning a tug came alongside and towed us up the Bay, past the Statue of Liberty and up the North River to Yonkers, where dock space was ready, and we warped the ship into it. All the crimps who had met us in Tottenville were at the dock as a reception committee. As soon as the ship was moored and the gangway put aboard, they came pouring on deck, buttonholing the sailors, stuffing cigars into their mouths, and generally claiming them as their own.

A plug-ugly came up to me, hail fellow well met, and claimed me as one who had promised to come to his boardinghouse. When I replied I didn't know him from Adam, he asked sourly, why did I take his cigars and liquor if I meant to welch on my promises. It ended for the time being when I told him, in no uncertain terms, to leave me alone. I hated their breed and my dander was rising. A few minutes later, with the whole crew busy on deck, another sailor and I were making things shipshape on the focs'lehead when I saw the same fellow enter the empty focs'le and I saw red. I jumped off the focs'lehead, threw a coiled jibsheet off its belaying pin, yanked the pin out of the rail and went into the focs'le after him, demanding:

"Where do you think you are? Get the hell out of here, and stay out!" He looked astonished.

"It's all right, Jack. Keep your shirt on. I'm not trying to steal anything."

But I was beside myself with rage. "Get out, you've no business in here alone. Get out or I'll crack your head open for you," I said, brandishing the belaying pin. "I don't like your kind."

He must have thought me crazy, and went out on deck to join some of his pals, and judging by the glances they directed at me, I must have been the subject of their conversation.

When the ship was properly moored, and the tarpaulin taken off the hatches, we all went back to the focs'le, and the crimps departed, promising to be back in the evening to take us to New York. We had our last supper of tea and hardtack and the fellows dressed in their shore clothes, ready to follow the crimps and make a night of it. I thought it best to stay aboard that night. Fatty Ecklund had warned me that he had overheard some of the crimps saying that that Dutch bastard was going to get his, if they got hold of him off the ship. I didn't relish the idea of being beaten up in some dark side street, and I heeded Ecklund's advice and spent the last night aboard the *Gwydyr Castle* all alone but for two of the apprentices who alternated as night watchmen.

In the morning I packed my seabag and stepped off the gangplank, bound for the British Consulate in downtown New York to be paid off. My shipmates were already there, most of them showing the evidences of having spent a lurid first night on shore, and some of them were rather riled up. It seemed that all of us who had originally signed on in Hamburg were to pay a bonus of two months' wages to the owners for the privilege of being paid off at the end of two years instead of three, for which we had signed on. It was a scurvy trick, but we agreed to it, and I at least gladly. With my pay in my pocket I left the *Gwydyr Castle* behind and went to the Episcopal Seaman's Mission at 52 Market Street, which was to be my home for the next three years. Occasionally in the following week I ran across some of my old shipmates down along Cherry and Water Streets and the last news I had of the *Gwydyr Castle* was that she was bound for Newcastle, Australia, with a cargo of case oil.

Thus ended my two years' voyage aboard a British limejuicer. I found the Episcopal Mission very pleasant. I had no real plans for the future, though by this time I was twenty-one years of age and due to return to Germany for my four years' service in the German Navy. I wasn't any too anxious to begin it and went down to the German Consulate on Bowling Green to ask for a year's *Ausstand* or leave of absence.

I went to the Consulate wearing a cheap suit, turtleneck sweater and a visored cap, looking like the sailor that I was. After waiting for some time in an anteroom, I was called into an office where I voiced my request. The young official interrogating me recognized my low social status and became supercilious and arrogant in his questioning. Suddenly it came over me that I was through with all that sort of thing, looked the fellow straight in the eye, and told him to go to hell.

I walked out of the office and out of the Consulate without a backward glance, and returned to the Seaman's Mission, thus ending one chapter of my life. Two days afterward I applied for my first papers for American citizenship, which marked the beginning of a new one.

AFTERWORD

"But what happened next?"—That has always been the question readers of *Focs'le Days*' first edition asked. No doubt it will arise again in the wake of this new (and I am happy to say: colorful edition), so here is a brief summary of the ensuing years. Those interested in a fuller account can find it in *Anton Otto Fischer—Marine Artist*, the biography I did in collaboration with Alex Hurst, a British nautical authority.

It was 1902 when the new chapter in AOF's life began and for the first couple of years he followed the only trade he knew: that of a sailor, racing as a yacht-hand in the summertime and teaching seamanship on the old Schoolship St. Mary's in the winter. Then Fate made one of its right-angled turns, and he answered an ad for model and handy man with the illustrator A.B. Frost. Frost recognized AOF's talent and was instrumental in convincing him to go and study in Paris, where Frost was taking his own two boys. After two years at the Académie Julian, AOF returned to the United States in 1908 and began the young illustrator's struggle to get established. Fate stepped in again—and he was teamed up as illustrator with Jack London, who was at the height of his popularity.

During the first World War AOF had the usual problems of a German in the United States. He couldn't earn a living in New York City and moved up to the Catskill Mountains where he spent most of the rest of his life. In 1912 he married Mary Ellen Sigsbee, also a struggling young illustrator whom he had first met in Paris. They bought an old farmhouse near Shandaken, NY as a summer home, to which they moved perma-nently in 1917. AOF's first papers had been stolen in Paris, but his citizenship was rushed through. His wife, however, who was the daughter of Admiral C.D. Sigsbee, the Captain in command of the battleship Maine when it was blown up in Havana harbor, found herself a subject of the Kaiser when the 1920 census was taken!

By the 1920s AOF was an established illustrator, and by the 1930s well-known as a marine painter. So much so, that in the 1940s with World War II, the U.S. Coast Guard asked him to be their Artist Laureate and con-ferred the rank of Lieutenant Commander on him. In the winter of 1943 he went on active duty in the North Atlantic Convoy Patrol, serving aboard the U.S.C.G. Cutter Campbell, and returned to paint a stirring series of paintings depicting what the convoys were facing in the North Atlantic. These appeared in *Life Magazine* and were exhibited at the Corcoran Gallery in Washington as well as around the country by the Coast Guard.

Focs'le Days was created in 1946, and was published by Charles Scribners & Sons in 1947. In 1949 AOF had a coronary from which he made a full recovery, but after-wards he gave up commercial illustrating almost entirely—he had worked too long under the strain of a deadline not to feel pressured. He remained busy in his studio, however, right up to the time he died at the age of 80, working in his garden in the spring of 1962.

Katrina Sigsbee Fischer 1987

THE GWYDYR CASTLE

THE GWYDYR CASTLE
A Water Color Done by AOF in 1901 or 1902

This bit of AOF's juvenilia was an interesting spin-off from the biography of him I did which was published in England in 1977. In the winter of 1979 I received a letter from a German doctor whose hobby was collecting "Kapitänsbilder" or ship's portraits. He had come across a copy of the book and immediately made the connection between *Anton Otto Fischer—Marine Artist* and a little water color of the *Gwydyr Castle* signed "Otto Fischer," which he had acquired from the son of a German sea captain who had died in 1965, a connection he had had verified by Dr. Jürgen Meyer of the Altonaer Museum in Hamburg. To confirm the matter even further, the sea captain's name was Paul Bergholz—the name of the "other German" who had signed on the *Gwydyr Castle* with AOF in Hamburg in 1901.

The good doctor enclosed an excellent photo of the little painting (it is only 10″ × 6¼″) and of another which, although unsigned, was certainly more of AOF's juvenilia. I was fascinated by this long arm of historical coincidence reaching out over the years. It settles once and for all the moot question of whether AOF did any painting as a sailor—a question on which even he contradicted himself. He always said he did not; but on the other hand, in *Focs'le Days* he tells of his ship mates suggesting him to the photographer in Tacoma as someone who could produce a painting of the *Gwydyr Castle* as a substitute for the photo the photographer had failed to get!

Captain Bergholz must have had the little painting amongst his effects for quite a while before he got back to Hamburg, and I've felt very grateful to him for the good care he took of it.

Katrina Sigsbee Fischer 1987

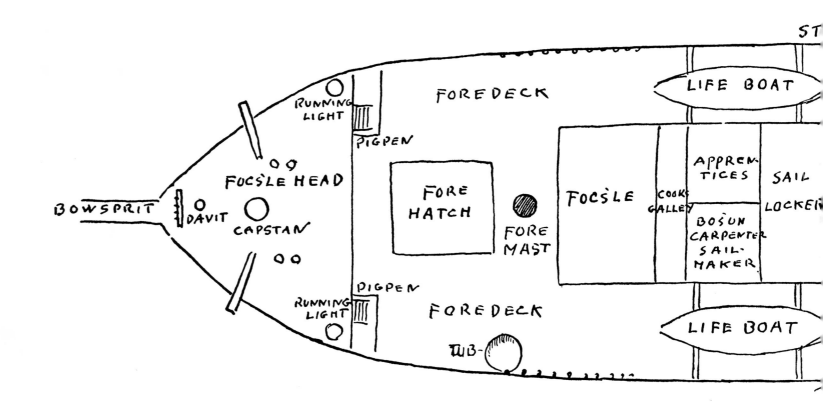

DECK PLAN OF THE GWYDYR CASTLE

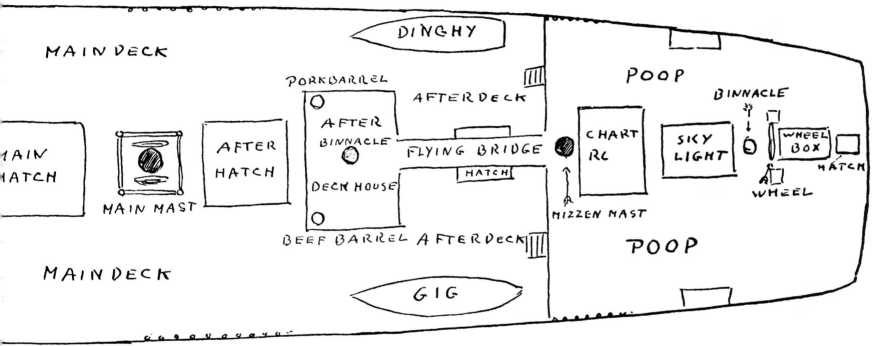

RD SIDE

MAIN DECK

DINGHY

PORKBARREL

AFTERDECK

MAIN HATCH

AFTER HATCH

AFTER BINNACLE

FLYING BRIDGE

HATCH

DECK HOUSE

MAIN MAST

BEEF BARREL AFTERDECK

MAIN DECK

GIG

POOP

BINNACLE

CHART RC

SKY LIGHT

WHEEL BOX

HATCH

WHEEL

MIZZEN MAST

POOP

IDE